PINPOINT
KELLER & RUTZ

Bruno Keller & Stephan Rutz

PINPOINT
KEY FACTS + FIGURES FOR
SUSTAINABLE BUILDINGS

Birkhäuser
Basel

vdf
Zurich

100611991 2

PREFACE

Sustainable construction today means the design and realization of buildings offering a high standard of comfort to the user, alongside durability and only the minimum of energy demands.

This means:
→ high thermal comfort,
→ ample daylight,
→ good sound protection against external as well as internal sources of noise,
→ good room acoustics,
→ no problems of condensation and mould growth,
→ a low enough energy demand that softer and more efficient methods can be used to cover it.

To fulfil all these requirements seems difficult, at least at first sight. The many textbooks on building physics and on HVAC systems now on the market, together with the many EN standards, can create more confusion than clarification for the practitioner.

For this reason, the authors present here the critical aspects of sustainable construction, with the necessary formulae and tables, illustrated by examples.

The fundamental laws and equations are universal. The calculations, examples, standard values and climate data given here, however, mostly use Swiss values and standards. The examples demonstrate how the equations can be used, and the reader can substitute country-specific data.

This book does not replace textbooks and published standards, but is intended to help designers with a background in this field to work more efficiently, by focusing on the most relevant points.

In addition there are software tools available on www.pinpoint-online.ch, such as the Energy Design Guide. Their use will help optimize energy efficiency even in the early phases of building design.

The authors have reaped the benefit of discussions with and significant contributions from many colleagues, and therefore we express our thanks and deep appreciation to all.

Bruno Keller and Stephan Rutz

ENERGY IN BUILDING

COMFORT CONDITIONS FOR INTERIOR SPACES

PERCEPTION OF HEAT AND REACTION

Warm threshold 37 °C
Central perception
Heat sensors in the brain → reaction if core temperature of the human body rises above 37 °C

Universal reaction by sweating to get rid of excess heat through evaporation

Cold threshold 34 °C
Peripheral perception
Cold sensors in the skin → reaction if the skin temperature falls below 34 °C

Local reaction by reduction of the blood supply, activation of local muscles (trembling)

MOST IMPORTANT COMFORT FACTORS

Comfort range of the room temperature
20 °C $\leq \theta_i \leq$ 26 °C
Temperatures above the comfort range: inactivity, reduced intellectual capability

The nearer the temperature is to the upper limit of the comfort range, the more sensitive humans are to deviations from the ideal value.

Temperatures below the comfort range: adaptation by suitable clothing

A **Comfort diagram**
Shows the sensitivity of the human body to surrounding temperatures and its tolerance of discomfort: ± °C

B **Temperature of the surrounding surfaces**
→ less than 3 K below room air temperature
→ greater differences lead to draught and radiation loss towards cold surfaces

Fresh air
for breathing and hygiene
air change, comfort ventilation*

Humidity
30–60% relative humidity recommended
best for breathing

Moisture*
Prevention of mould growth and condensation problems

Daylight*
provide adequate natural room illumination

Sound*
Protection against internal and external noise impact

Room acoustics*
keep the correct reverberation time

* see corresponding chapters

A Comfort Diagram

Comfort range 20–26 °C, ± °C: sensitivity to differences

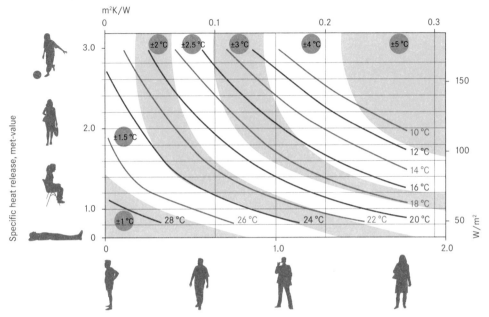

Specific heat release, met-value

Thermal resistance of clothing, clo-value

B Temperature of surrounding surfaces

Discomfort due to radiation asymmetry

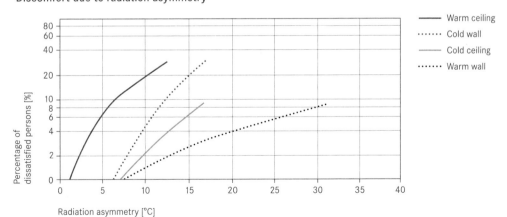

Percentage of dissatisfied persons [%]

Radiation asymmetry [°C]

—— Warm ceiling
········ Cold wall
—— Cold ceiling
········ Warm wall

HUMAN REFERENCE FIGURES

Body size
1.7 m, 69 kg
at rest

Height	1.70 m
Weight	69 kg
Surface	1.7 m²
Volume	0.07 m³
Body core temperature	37 °C
Skin temperature	34 °C
Breathing volume	up to 0.5 m³/h
Number of breaths	16/min
Pulse	60–80/min
CO₂ production	10–20 dm³/h
H₂O release	40 g/h

met-VALUE
HUMAN POWER RELEASE
mean heat flux density q across body surface

$$q = \frac{\dot{Q}}{A} = \frac{100}{1.7} = 58.8 \left[\frac{W}{m^2}\right] = 1 \text{ met} \left[\frac{W}{m^2}\right]$$

1 met = heat release of a person sitting quietly
q: Heat flux density [W/m²]
$\dot{Q}$: Heat flux [W]
A: Body surface [m²]

Activity	Total heat release		
	$\dot{Q}$ [W/Prs.]*	q [W/m²]	met [W/m²]
Lying quietly	83	46	0.8
Sitting quietly	100	59	1.0
Standing relaxedly	126	70	1.2
Work, sitting (office, school, living)	126	70	1.2
Light work, standing (shop, light bench work)	167	93	1.6
Medium heavy work (sales, house-hold, work bench)	209	116	2.0
Walking 2 km/h 3 km/h 4 km/h 5 km/h	198 250 292 355	110 140 165 200	1.9 2.4 2.8 3.4
Heavy work	313	174	3.0

* valid for a person of: height 1.7 m, weight 69 kg, body surface 1.7 m²

clo-VALUE
HEAT TRANSMISSION RESISTANCE
OF CLOTHING
1 clo = 0.155 m²K/W
heat transmission resistance of clothing with underwear, shirt, trousers, jacket, socks, shoes
see pages 14–15

Heat transmission resistance R [m²K/W]

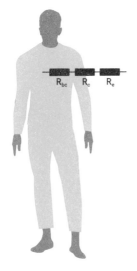

$R_{tot} = R_{bc} + R_c + R_e$

at
body temperature 37 °C
skin temperature 34 °C
sitting quietly 59 W/m²

Heat transmission resistance of the body:

$R_{bc} = \dfrac{37-34}{59} = \dfrac{3}{59} = 0.051 \text{ m}^2\text{K/W}$

Body core to skin

R_c = Heat transmission resistance of clothing according to table

$R_e = 0.125 \text{ m}^2\text{K/W}$
Heat transfer resistance from clothing to environment

Relationship between clo-value and met-value

Example
Body core temperature $\theta_{bc} = 37$ °C
Air temperature of room $\theta = 22$ °C

Clothing:
shirt, trousers, jacket, socks, shoes
1.0 clo $\cong R_c = 0.155 \text{ m}^2\text{K/W}$

Heat flux density for discharging the body
light work, standing
1.6 met $\cong q = 93 \text{ W/m}^2$

Heat flux density across clothing

$q = \dfrac{\Delta\theta}{R_{bc} + R_c + R_e}$

$q = \dfrac{15}{0.052 + 0.155 + 0.125} = 48 \text{ W/m}^2$

Heat release needed is greater than the flux across the clothing
93 W/m² > 48 W/m²
Body will overheat

Reaction possibilities:
Decrease R_c (clothing)
Change room temperature
Change activity

clo-VALUE DAILY WEAR CLOTHING

	clo-value	R_c [m²K/W]
Underwear, T-shirt, shorts, light socks, sandals	0.30	0.05
Underwear, slip, stockings, light dress with sleeves, sandals	0.45	0.07
Underwear, shirt with short sleeves, light trousers, light socks, shoes	0.50	0.08
Underwear, stockings, shirt with short sleeves, skirt, sandals	0.55	0.085
Underwear, shirt, lightweight trousers, socks, shoes	0.60	0.095
Underwear, slip, stockings, dress, shoes	0.70	0.105
Underwear, shirt, trousers, socks, shoes	0.70	0.11
Underwear, track suit (sweater and trousers), long socks, trainers	0.75	0.115
Underwear, slip, shirt, skirt, thick knee-socks, shoes	0.80	0.12
Underwear, shirt, skirt, round-neck sweater, thick knee-socks, shoes	0.90	0.14
Underpants, singlet with short sleeves, shirt, trousers, V-neck sweater, socks, shoes	0.95	0.145
Underwear, shirt, trousers, jacket, socks, shoes	1.00	0.155
Underwear, stockings, shirt, skirt, waistcoat, jacket	1.00	0.155
Underwear, stockings, blouse, long skirt, jacket, shoes	1.10	0.17
Underwear, singlet with short sleeves, shirt, trousers, jacket, socks, shoes	1.10	0.17
Underwear, singlet with short sleeves, shirt, trousers, waistcoat, jacket, socks, shoes	1.15	0.18
Underwear with long sleeves and legs, shirt, trousers, V-neck sweater, jacket, socks, shoes	1.30	0.20
Underwear with short sleeves and legs, shirt, trousers, waistcoat, coat, socks, shoes	1.50	0.23

clo-VALUE WORK CLOTHING

	clo-value	R_b [m²K/W]
Underwear, boiler suit, socks, shoes	0.70	0.11
Underwear, shirt, trousers, socks, shoes	0.75	0.115
Underwear, shirt, trousers, boiler suit, socks, shoes	0.80	0.125
Underwear, shirt, trousers, jacket, socks, shoes	0.85	0.135
Underwear, shirt, trousers, smock, socks, shoes	0.90	0.14
Underwear with short sleeves and legs, shirt, trousers, jacket, socks, shoes	1.00	0.155
Underwear with short sleeves and legs, trousers, boiler suit, socks, shoes	1.10	0.17
Underwear with long sleeves and legs, thermojacket, socks, shoes	1.20	0.185
Underwear with short sleeves and legs, shirt, trousers, jacket, thermojacket, socks, shoes	1.25	0.19
Underwear with short sleeves and legs, boiler suit, thermojacket and trousers, socks, shoes	1.40	0.22
Underwear with short sleeves and legs, shirt, trousers, jacket, thermojacket and trousers, socks, shoes	1.55	0.225
Underwear with short sleeves and legs, shirt, trousers, jacket, heavy quilted outer jacket and overalls, socks, shoes	1.85	0.285
Underwear with short sleeves and legs, shirt, trousers, jacket, heavy quilted outer jacket and overalls, socks, shoes, cap, gloves	2.00	0.31
Underwear with long sleeves and legs, thermojacket and trousers, outer thermojacket and trousers, socks, shoes	2.20	0.34
Underwear with long sleeves and legs, thermojacket and trousers, Parka with heavy quilting, overalls with heavy quilting, socks, shoes, cap, gloves	2.55	0.395

CLIMATE INFLUENCE

A EXTERNAL AIR TEMPERATURE θ_e [°C, k]

With periodic components
Day, in a first approximation:
Daily mean value: $\bar{\theta}_d$
Daily variation (amplitude):
$\Delta\theta_d \approx$ 2–10 K
Daily maximum/minimum:
$\bar{\theta}_d \pm \Delta\theta_d$

Year, in a first approximation:
Yearly mean value:
$\bar{\theta}_y \approx$ 9 °C (Switzerland...)
Yearly variation (amplitude):
$\Delta\theta_y \approx$ 13–14 K

Generally:
Temperature range of external air temperature
$$\theta_{e,\,min,\,max} = \underbrace{\bar{\theta}_y \pm \Delta\theta_y}_{\bar{\theta}_d} \pm \Delta\theta_d$$

With random component
Weather

A EXTERNAL AIR TEMPERATURE θ_e [°C, k]
Overview of temperature distribution, e.g. Switzerland

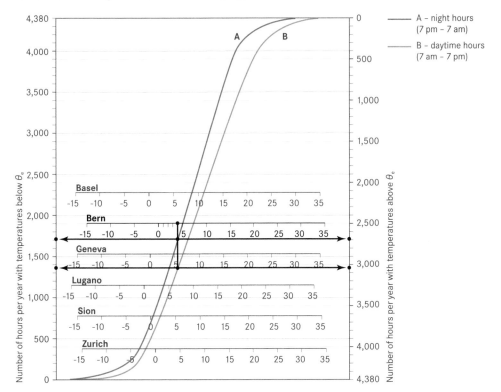

Frequency of external temperature θ_e for day and night times, yearly
e.g. Bern at 4 °C

$\theta_e \leq 4\ °C$	Night hours 1,700 h	Daytime hours 1,350 h
$\theta_e \geq 4\ °C$	Night hours 2,680 h	Daytime hours 3,030 h

B SOLAR IRRADIATION I [W/m²]

With periodic components
mean value: $\bar{I}$
variation (amplitude): ΔI
maximum/minimum: $\bar{I} \pm \Delta I$

With random component
Weather

SOLAR RADIATION
corresponds approximately to the radiation
emitted by a black body of 6,000 K.

**Spectral distribution of the vertical
incident solar radiation**
4% ultraviolet
56% visible light
40% infrared

**Power density of the total
solar irradiation I_{max} [W/m²]**
on the external atmosphere $\approx$ 1,370 W/m²
on the earth's surface, depending on the
weather

Three groups of solar irradiation intensity
with different ratios of direct and/or diffuse
radiation

Attention should be paid to:

C Frequency distribution
of the radiation intensity to estimate the
available power density

B SOLAR IRRADIATION I [W/m²]
on the earth's surface, depending on the weather

cool, clear blue sky	thick haze	sun breaks through	yellow disc	white disc	sun dis-cernible	stratus	covered sky

Global radiation

1,000 W/m²	500 W/m²	500 W/m²	400 W/m²	300 W/m²	200 W/m²	100 W/m²	50 W/m²

Diffusive percentage

10%	50%	30%	50%	60%	100%	100%	100%

C Frequency distribution
Example: Swiss Plateau in winter
Time span: November to February, because of stratus

Power density I :

Intensities above 100 W/m²	100 to 150 h per month	approx. 14–22%
Intensities below 100 W/m²	remaining hours of the month	570–620 h

Sun frequency
Example: Zurich airport, 1986

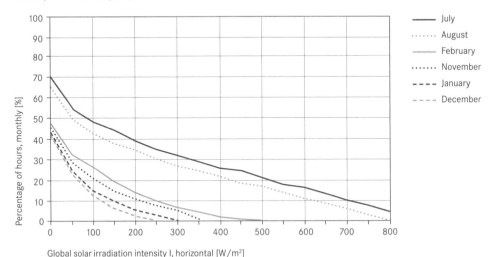

Global solar irradiation intensity I, horizontal [W/m²]

Legend:
— July
······· August
— February
······· November
--- January
--- December

Monthly change in sun angles
The slight variation in the earth's axis is ignored
Example: Zurich

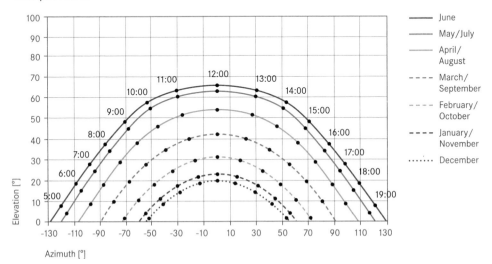

Azimuth [°]

Legend:
— June
— May/July
— April/August
--- March/September
--- February/October
--- January/November
······· December

Total solar irradiation I
July, 50° north, atmosphere of a large city
on walls north, south, east, west
on the horizontal plane
on the normal plane: plane perpendicular to the direction of the sun

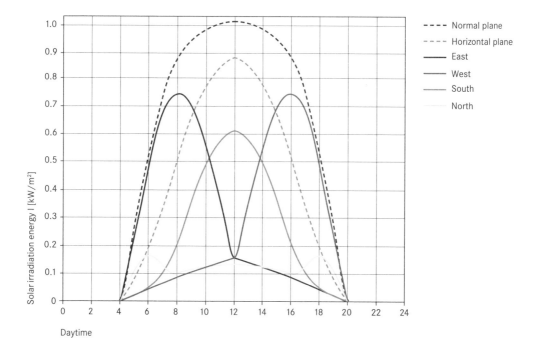

Daytime

Diffuse solar irradiation I
January, 50° north, large city atmosphere

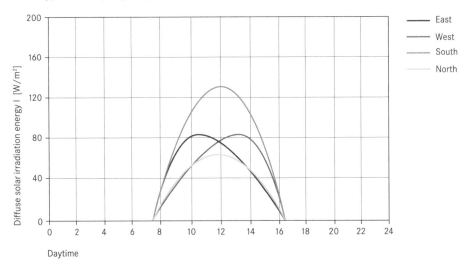

East
West
South
North

Diffuse solar irradiation energy I [W/m²]

Daytime

Diffuse solar irradiation I
July, 50° north, large city atmosphere

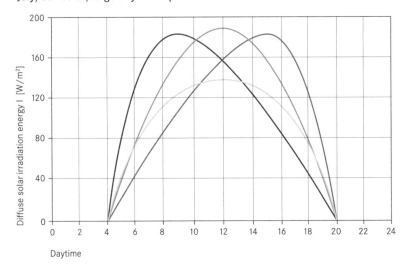

Diffuse solar irradiation energy I [W/m²]

Daytime

D SOLAR IRRADIATION I [W/m²]
Approximate determination
The mean and maximum daily solar irradiation I,
together with the sunshine duration, are
sufficient for the basic considerations and
calculations for a building.

Daily mean value $\overline{I}$
$$\overline{I} = \frac{a_0}{2} \cdot I_{max} \ [W/m^2]$$

Daily amplitude ΔI_d
$$\Delta I_d = |a_1| \cdot I_{max} \ [W/m^2]$$

Relevant daily maximum I_{max}
for T = 24 h
$$I_{max} = \overline{I} + \Delta I \ [W/m^2]$$

Fourier components $a_0/2$ and a_1
applicable for the computation of the irradiation intensity I as a function of the sunshine
duration t

D SOLAR IRRADIATION I [W/m²]
  Approximate determination:
  Fourier components $a_0/2$ and a_1

Solar irradiation approximate computation of	Mean value $\bar{I}$ for 24 h	1. Amplitude, fundamental frequency of irradiation
Fourier components	$a_0/2$	$|a_1|$
Duration of sunshine t [h]		
4	0.111	0.215
6	0.165	0.310
8	0.218	0.391
10	0.269	0.455
12	0.318	0.500
14	0.364	0.527
16	0.406	0.536
18	0.443	0.533
20	0.472	0.520
22	0.492	0.507

SOLAR IRRADIATION I
Computation of mean value and daily amplitude

Example
daily maximum I_{max} = 600 W/m²
duration of sunshine t = 16 h

Daily mean value $\bar{I}$

$\bar{I} = \dfrac{a_0}{2} \cdot I_{max} = 0.406 \cdot 600 = 243.6$ W/m²

The daily mean value of the solar irradiation
is relevant for the stationary part of the heat exchange,
as it determines the energy need for cooling.

Daily amplitude ΔI_d

$\Delta I_d = |a_1| \cdot I_{max} = 0.536 \cdot 600 = 321.6$ W/m²

The daily amplitude of the solar irradiation
is relevant for non-stationary part of the heat exchange,
as it determines the required peak cooling power.

Relevant daily maximum I_{max}
$I_{max} = \bar{I} + \Delta I = 243.6 + 321.6 = 565.2$ W/m²

MONTHLY MEAN VALUES OF EXTERNAL TEMPERATURE $\bar{\theta}_e$ [°C] AND GLOBAL IRRADIATION G IN kWh/m²

Basel

Month/ location	°C	G_H	G_S	G_N	$G_{E,W}$
1	0.3	32	51	18	10
2	1.1	48	61	25	12
3	5.0	88	87	48	21
4	8.6	122	84	63	27
5	13.3	160	84	79	34
6	16.6	165	77	81	37
7	18.4	166	83	79	34
8	17.2	135	86	70	28
9	14.9	112	100	61	21
10	9.7	68	84	41	15
11	4.9	34	51	21	7
12	0.7	25	44	15	8

Lausanne

Month/ Location	°C	G_H	G_S	G_N	$G_{E,W}$
1	0.7	29	46	16	9
2	1.7	49	62	25	13
3	5.3	100	97	54	24
4	9.0	128	87	66	28
5	13.9	173	91	85	36
6	17.1	182	85	89	41
7	18.9	176	88	83	36
8	17.6	157	100	82	33
9	15.4	115	103	63	22
10	10.2	72	89	44	16
11	5.3	31	47	19	7
12	1.8	26	45	16	8

Bern

Month/ location	°C	G_H	G_S	G_N	$G_{E,W}$
1	-1.5	32	52	18	11
2	0.2	52	65	27	13
3	4.0	97	95	52	23
4	8.2	124	85	64	27
5	12.4	161	84	79	34
6	16.2	164	77	80	37
7	17.6	180	90	86	37
8	17.0	148	94	77	31
9	14.7	111	99	61	21
10	8.9	70	86	42	15
11	4.1	30	45	18	6
12	0.1	23	40	14	7

Lugano

Month/ Location	°C	G_H	G_S	G_N	$G_{E,W}$
1	2.2	41	66	23	13
2	3.9	60	76	31	15
3	7.5	90	88	49	22
4	11.5	135	92	69	29
5	15.7	168	88	83	35
6	19.0	182	85	89	41
7	21.4	190	95	90	39
8	20.6	161	102	84	34
9	17.7	116	104	64	22
10	12.5	84	103	51	18
11	7.1	41	62	25	9
12	3.6	32	56	19	10

Conversion: 1 kWh = 3.6 MJ

G_H Irradiation on horizontal
G_S Irradiation on vertical south
G_N Irradiation on vertical north
$G_{E,W}$ Irradiation on vertical east, west
for further locations see annex

Month/ location	°C	G_H	G_S	G_N	$G_{E,W}$

Davos

1	-6.4	46	74	25	15
2	-5.8	66	83	34	17
3	-2.6	115	113	62	28
4	2.0	147	101	76	32
5	7.0	169	89	83	35
6	10.6	162	76	79	36
7	12.3	173	87	82	35
8	11.5	143	90	74	30
9	9.5	112	101	62	21
10	4.1	85	105	51	19
11	-0.7	52	78	32	11
12	-4.7	37	64	22	12

La-Chaux-de-Fonds

1	-1.1	32	51	18	10
2	-0.1	48	61	25	12
3	2.4	93	91	50	22
4	5.9	124	85	64	27
5	10.5	161	84	79	34
6	13.8	158	73	77	35
7	15.8	165	83	79	34
8	14.6	139	88	72	29
9	12.6	109	97	60	21
10	8.2	75	93	45	17
11	3.4	38	57	23	8
12	0.2	27	48	17	9

Month/ location	°C	G_H	G_S	G_N	$G_{E,W}$

St. Gallen

1	-1.6	28	45	16	9
2	1.4	46	58	24	12
3	2.6	81	79	44	20
4	6.4	111	76	57	24
5	10.8	145	76	71	30
6	14.9	178	83	87	40
7	16.1	163	82	77	33
8	15.3	137	87	71	28
9	12.8	93	84	51	18
10	8.2	66	82	40	14
11	3.8	29	44	18	6
12	0.6	22	38	13	7

Zurich

1	-0.9	30	48	17	10
2	0.1	51	65	27	13
3	4.5	102	100	55	25
4	8.3	123	84	63	27
5	12.6	164	86	81	34
6	15.6	170	79	83	38
7	17.7	170	86	81	35
8	16.5	146	93	76	30
9	14.4	119	107	66	23
10	9.1	70	86	42	15
11	4.1	31	46	19	7
12	0.5	22	38	13	7

BASIC MECHANISMS OF HEAT TRANSFER

EXTERIOR ENVIRONMENT: INFRARED RADIATION – RADIATION EXCHANGE

between a building and its environment, and with the air (several km thickness of air layer)

Heat transfer coefficient h_r for external infrared radiation
h_r = 4.4–5.1 W/m²K

Radiation balance
with sky cover (clouds, fog)
The radiation temperature of the atmospheric radiation corresponds to the air temperature.

"Radiation hole"
Partial permeability of the clear atmosphere to thermal infrared radiation:
External surfaces irradiate much more to the cold space than they receive. The surface temperature decreases below air temperature. This can result in an increased heating demand of up to 20% over the year.

CONVECTION – CONVECTION TRANSFER

dominates the energy balance externally, caused by wind or by strong convection flux due to large temperature differences on the surfaces.

Heat transfer coefficient h_c for external convection
$h_c = 8.1 \cdot v^{0.6}$ W/m²K
v: Air velocity, wind speed [m/s]

TOTAL EFFECT OF RADIATION AND CONVECTION

Radiation and convection ratios are combined into an external heat transfer coefficient h_e:

External heat transfer coefficient h_e
SIA Switzerland/DIN Germany
h_e = 25.0 W/m²K

ASHRAE USA
Winter
h_e = 34.1 W/m²K
Summer
h_e = 22.7 W/m²K

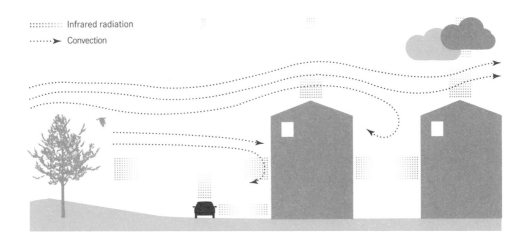

A INTERIOR SPACES:
INFRARED RADIATION –
RADIATION EXCHANGE
Energy exchange by means of electromagnetic
waves from each surface:
"Sensation of warmth" near to a surface at
room temperature

Wavelength for maximum intensity: 10 μm

Heat radiation dominates the heat transfer
internally

Heat transfer coefficient h_r
for radiation inside a room
h_r = 4.4–5.1 W/m²K

Temperature
The higher the temperature, the stronger the
radiation emitted and the shorter the wavelengths of maximum intensity.

Incident radiation intensity
depends on:
geometry, distance, surface material and
texture (emissivity) of the surroundings and
their temperature.

Radiation deficit
A warm body emits more heat than it receives
from cool or cold environment: local cooling,
"feeling of draught".

HEAT CONDUCTION AND CONVECTION
Heating or cooling of air layers near to surfaces by conduction, i.e. direct contact

This creates differences in density
within the ambient air.

A convection flow is induced and causes heat
transfer.

Heat transfer coefficient h_c
for natural convection inside a room
h_c = 1.5–2 W/m²K

A INTERIOR ROOM:
INFRARED RADIATION, HEAT CONDUCTION AND CONVECTION

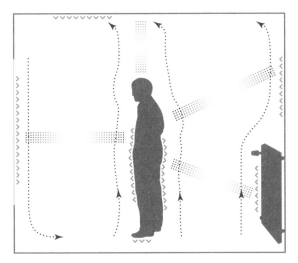

:::::::::::: Infrared radiation

·······➤ Convection

∧∧∧∧ Heat conduction

BOUNDARY LAYER
Sliding air layer caused by a temperature difference between air and a surface, especially in front of glazed openings.
Ambient air is cooled down by conduction, and sinks. Thickness of boundary layers approx. 0.2 m

Magnitude of boundary layer flow – depends on the geometry and surface temperature differences (glazing). Its speed is decisive in determining comfort.

Falling speed of the boundary layer should be less than v < 0.3 m/s to maintain the comfort level.

B CONVECTION FLOW = BOUNDARY LAYER FLOW
The greater the temperature difference $\Delta\theta$ between ambient air and inner surface, and the higher the glazed opening, the stronger the convection flow.

TOTAL COMBINED EFFECT OF RADIATION AND CONVECTION
merge into an internal heat transfer coefficient h_i.

Internal heat transfer coefficient h_i
SIA Switzerland
$h_i = 8$ W/m^{2}K or $h_i = 6$ W/m^{2}K
see also pages 36–37

In interior spaces, the heat transfer by radiation is about twice as intensive as transfer by natural convection: → relevant for comfort

Determining factors
for the prevention of radiation deficit "sensation of draught"

→ **Glazing height h**

→ **U_g-value of glazing**
dependent on its height h and the external temperature θ_e

B CONVECTION FLOW = BOUNDARY LAYER FLOW

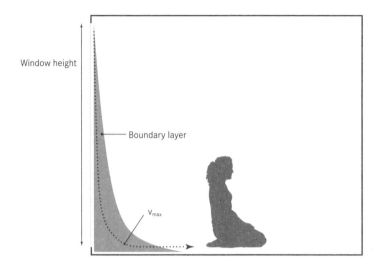

Maximum flow speed v_{max} of the boundary layer

as function of temperature difference between ambient air and surface temperature of the glazing and height of glazing h.

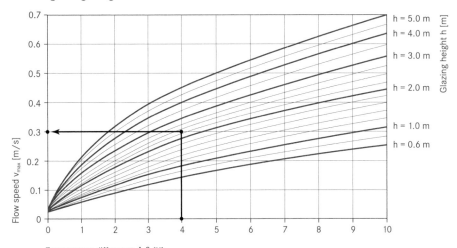

Flow speed v_{max} [m/s]

Temperature difference $\Delta\theta$ [K]

h = 5.0 m
h = 4.0 m
h = 3.0 m
h = 2.0 m
h = 1.0 m
h = 0.6 m

Glazing height h [m]

Maximum allowable U_g-value of glazing
to prevent feeling a draught and to maintain a flow speed v < 0.3 m/s in function of the glazing's height h

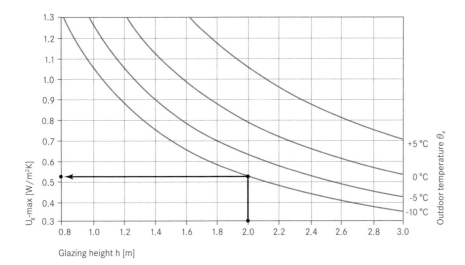

U_g-max [W/m²K]

Glazing height h [m]

Outdoor temperature θ_e

STATIONARY HEAT EXCHANGE

Temperature difference $\Delta\theta$: Constant $\neq 0$
Heat flux $\dot{Q}$: Constant $\neq 0$
Thermal state: Balanced flow

$$q = \frac{\dot{Q}}{A} = \frac{\Delta\theta}{R} = \frac{\lambda}{d} \cdot \Delta\theta \quad [W/m^2]$$

with:
q: Heat flow density $[W/m^2]$
$\dot{Q}$: Heat flux [W]
A: Surface area to be considered $[m^2]$
$\Delta\theta$: Temperature difference [K]
$R = \frac{d}{\lambda}$: Heat transmission resistance $[m^2K/W]$
d: Thickness of material layer [m]
λ: Thermal conductivity of material [W/mK]

U-VALUE [W/m²K]

Measure of the heat throughput per m² and
1 K temperature difference

$$U = \frac{1}{R_{tot}} = \frac{1}{\dfrac{1}{h_i} + R_{wall} + \dfrac{1}{h_e}}$$

U	Heat transmission coefficient	[W/m²K]
h_i, h_e	Heat transfer coefficients	[W/m²K]

the lower the U-value, the less heat transmitted

A Heat transfer coefficients for basic computation

Interior – detailed

Convection	Radiation
$h_c \approx 1.5–2.5$ W/m²K	$h_r \approx 4–5$ W/m²K

Interior – overall

Convection + radiation
$h_i \approx 8$ W/m²K

Exterior – detailed

Convection	Radiation
$h_c \approx 8.1 \cdot V^{0.6}$ W/m²K	$h_r \approx 5$ W/m²K

Exterior – overall

Convection + radiation
$h_e \approx 25$ W/m²K

A Heat transfer coefficients for basic computations

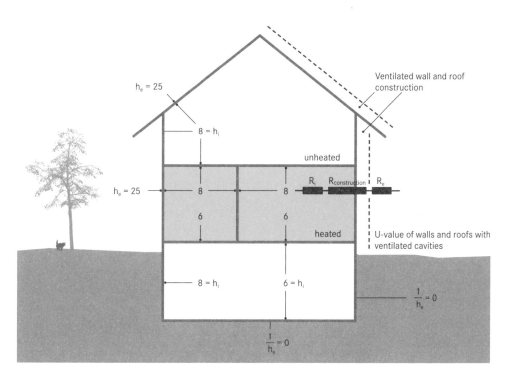

Heat transfer coefficients for ventilated wall and roof constructions
Air layer open on top and at the bottom, heat transmission of air layer negligible; the external heat transfer coefficient h_e is lowered to the value of the internal coefficient h_i.

U-value of ventilated wall and roof constructions

$$U = \frac{1}{R_{tot}} = \frac{1}{\dfrac{1}{h_i} + R_{wall} + \dfrac{1}{h_i}}$$

B COMPUTATION OF U-VALUE AND TEMPERATURE PROFILE

C Example: layers of construction

Outside temperature θ_e = -10 °C

Inside temperature θ_i = 20 °C

Layer structure from outside to inside

Material	Thickness [m]	λ [W/mK]
External plaster	0.01	0.87
Expanded polystyrene	0.12	0.038
Reinforced concrete	0.25	1.80
Internal plaster	0.01	0.70

Thermal conductivity λ [W/mK]
Specific material constant according to the layer structure

see table in the annex for material properties
see manufacturers' information

B COMPUTATION OF U-VALUE AND TEMPERATURE PROFILE

www.pinpoint-online.ch

U-value and temperature profile: computation table		Computation of heat transmission coefficient U, U-value					Computation of temperature profile		
		d	λ	$h_{e,i}$	$\dfrac{1}{h_{e,i}}$ or $\dfrac{d_j}{\lambda_j}$	$\dfrac{1}{h_{e,i}} + \sum_j \dfrac{d_j}{\lambda_j}$	q	$\Delta\theta$	θ
Set up	Material	[m]	[W/mK]	[W/m²K]	[m²K/W]	[m²K/W]	[W/m²]	[°C]	[°C]
External air		–	–	–	–		–	–	
External heat transfer		–	–	25	0.04	–	1) 5.92	2) 0.24	θ_e= -10.0
						0.04			θ_{se}= -9.76
1st layer	Plaster	0.01	0.87	–	0.011	0.051		3) 0.068	θ_{12}= -9.692
2nd layer	Polystyrene	0.18	0.038	–	4.737	4.788		3) 28.05	θ_{23}= 18.358
3rd layer	Concrete, reinf.	0.25	1.8	–	0.139	4.927		3) 0.82	θ_{34}= 19.172
4th layer	Stucco	0.01	0.7	–	0.014	4.941		3) 0.08	θ_{45}= 19.252
5th layer				–				3)	θ_{56}=
6th layer				–				3)	θ_{67}=
7th layer				–				3)	θ_{78}=
8th layer				–				3)	θ_{si}=
Internal heat transfer		–	–	8	0.125	5.066		2) 0.744	θ_i= 20.0
Internal air		–	–	–	–		–	–	

$$R_{tot} = \frac{1}{h_e} + \sum_j \frac{d_j}{\lambda_j} + \frac{1}{h_i} = 5.066 \quad [m^2K/W]$$

$$U = \frac{1}{R_{tot}} = 0.197 \quad [W/m^2K]$$

1) $q = U \cdot (\theta_i - \theta_e)$

2) $\Delta\theta = \dfrac{1}{h} \cdot q$

3) $\Delta\theta = \dfrac{d}{\lambda} \cdot q$

C Example: layers of construction

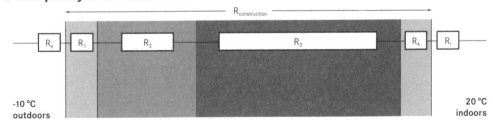

$R_{construction}$

R_e R_1 R_2 R_3 R_4 R_i

-10 °C outdoors

20 °C indoors

LOSS FACTOR F_L [W/K]
$F_L = F_{Ltr} + F_{Lac}$ [W/K]

D Loss factor F_{Ltr}
due to heat transmission
$F_{Ltr} = \sum_i A_i \cdot U_i + \sum_n I_n \cdot \chi_n + \sum_m \psi_m$ [W/K]

Areas $A_i \rightarrow$ with U-values U_i
linear bridges with length I_n
and linear correction $\chi_n{}^*$
point bridges with point corrections $\psi_m{}^*$
* see thermal bridges catalogues
Bundesamt für Energie, BFE, 2002

Loss factor F_{Lac}
due to air change
$F_{Lac} \cong \dfrac{n \cdot V}{3}$
see air infiltration

Heat loss P
$P = F_L \cdot \Delta\theta$ [W]

Example:

Loss factor F_{Ltr}
due to heat transmission
External surfaces
A_{wa} wall: 10 m², U_{wa}-value = 0.25 W/m²K
A_{wi} window: 4 m², U_{wi}-value = 1.1 W/m²K
Linear correction for window joint:
I_{wo} wall opening: 8.2 m, χ = 0.12 W/mK
Correction for fastening bolt:
2 pieces, each ψ = 0.3 W/K
$F_{Ltr} = A_{wa} \cdot U_{wa} + A_{wi} \cdot U_{wi} + I_{wo} \cdot \chi + 2 \cdot \psi$
$= 10 \cdot 0.25 + 4 \cdot 1.1 + 8.2 \cdot 0.12 + 2 \cdot 0.3$
$= 8.48$ W/K

Loss factor F_{Lac}
due to air change infiltration
room volume V: 60 m³
air exchange rate n: 0.5 h⁻¹
$F_{Lac} \cong \dfrac{n \cdot V}{3} = \dfrac{0.5 \cdot 60}{3} = 10$ W/K

Loss factor F_L
$F_L = F_{Ltr} + F_{Lac} = 8.48 + 10 = 18.48$ W/K

Heat loss P
mean room air temperature: 20 °C
external air temperature: -10 °C
$P = F_L \cdot \Delta\theta = 18.48 \cdot 30 = 554.4$ W
of which:
heat transmission 254.4 W
air infiltration 300 W

D Loss factor F_{Ltr} due to heat transmission
linear and point bridges

χ_n: linear corrections
ψ_n: point corrections

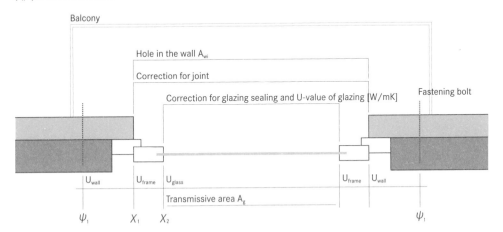

Balcony

Hole in the wall A_{wi}

Correction for joint

Correction for glazing sealing and U-value of glazing [W/mK]

Fastening bolt

U_{wall} U_{frame} U_{glass} U_{frame} U_{wall}

Transmissive area A_g

ψ_1 χ_1 χ_2 ψ_1

DESIGN PRINCIPLES FOR CONSTRUCTION

1. Place continuous layer of insulation around the building

2. Avoid hollow spaces connecting the warm to the cold side, to avoid radiation transfer and convection.

3. Avoid any metallic connections, if necessary limit to point connections.

4. Edges, corners and staggerings of the insulation layer require greater thickness or lower conductivity.

5. Bearing structure entirely on the warm side if possible. Cantilevers penetrating the insulation layer must be insulated as thoroughly as the facade.

6. Rigid insulation, (e.g. foam glass, rockwool, rigid polystyrene) can resist a distributed load but should not be subject to tensile or point loading.

7. For anchorages, use fibreglass or carbon reinforced plastics where possible. If metallic connections are used, limit to internal point connections separated from external metal sheeting: use plastic tubes or washers to secure adequate interior surface temperature to prevent condensation.

NON-STATIONARY/DYNAMIC HEAT EXCHANGE

Temperature difference $\Delta\theta$: variable
Heat flux q: variable

Heat flux and stored heat are variable under these conditions.

where:
ρ: Specific density [kg/m³]
c: Specific heat capacity [kJ/kgK]
$c \cdot \rho$: Specific volumetric heat capacity [kJ/m³K]
λ: Thermal conductivity [W/mK]

THERMAL CONDUCTANCE a [m²/s]
specific to each material

Measure of the temperature variation

$$a = \frac{\lambda}{c \cdot \rho} \; [m^2/s]$$

THERMAL ADMITTANCE b [kJ/m²Ks¹⁻²]
specific to each material

Measure of the amount of heat exchanged per time period: "in and out"

$$b = \sqrt{\lambda \cdot c \cdot \rho} \; \left[\frac{kJ}{m^2 \cdot K \cdot s^{\frac{1}{2}}} \right]$$

MATERIAL TABLE – CHARACTERISTIC DYNAMIC VALUES a, √a, b

Material	ρ [kg/m²]	c [kJ/kgK]	$c \cdot \rho$ [kJ/m²K]	λ [W/mK]	$a = \lambda/c \cdot \rho$ [10^{-8}m²/s]	$\sqrt{a} = \sqrt{\lambda/c \cdot \rho}$ [10^{-4}m/s$^{1/2}$]	$b = \sqrt{\lambda \cdot c \cdot \rho}$ [kJ/m²·K·s^{½}]
Clay	1,700	0.90	1,530	0.90	59	7.67	1.17
Sand/gravel	1,900	0.80	1,520	0.70	46	6.79	1.03
Brick	1,100	0.90	990	0.44	44	6.67	0.66
Optitherm	1,100	0.90	990	0.20	20	4.49	0.44
Lime brick	1,800	0.90	1,620	1.00	62	7.86	1.27
Aerated concrete	500	1.00	500	0.13	26	5.10	0.25
Reinforced concrete	2,400	1.10	2,640	1.80	68	8.26	2.18
Wood (spruce)	480	2.10	1,008	0.14	14	3.73	0.38
Pavatherm	approx. 215	2.70	580	0.06	10.34	3.22	0.19
Expanded polystyrene	17	1.40	24	0.04	167	12.91	0.03
Rockwool	approx. 80	0.60	48	0.04	83	9.11	1.38
Aluminium	2,700	0.90	2,430	200	8,230	90.72	22.05
Copper	8,900	0.39	3,471	380	10,948	104.63	36.31
Stainless steel	7,900	0.47	3,713	17	458	21.40	7.94
Glass	2,500	0.80	2,000	0.81	41	6.36	1.27
Hard rubber	1,200	1.42	1,704	0.16	9	3.06	0.52
Ice (< 0 °C)	860	2.05	1,763	2.23	126	11.25	1.98
Water (10 °C)	1,000	4.19	4,190	0.58	14	3.72	1.56
Air (still)	1.2	1.00	1.2	0.03	2,500	50.00	0.01

ρ: Specific density [kg/m³]
c: Specific heat capacity [kJ/kgK]
$c \cdot \rho$: Specific volumetric heat capacity [kJ/m³K]
λ: Thermal conductivity [W/mK]
a: Thermal conductance [10^{-8}m²/s]
b: Thermal admittance [kJ/m²·K·s^{½}]

**A PERIODIC EXCITATION =
TEMPERATURE WAVE**

Temperature variation penetrates the layer as a temperature wave: → the amplitude decreases with increasing material depth.

Phase shift

Delayed penetration of the temperature variation with increasing material depth

A **PERIODIC EXCITATION** = **TEMPERATURE WAVE**
phase shift

Example: temperature wave in concrete

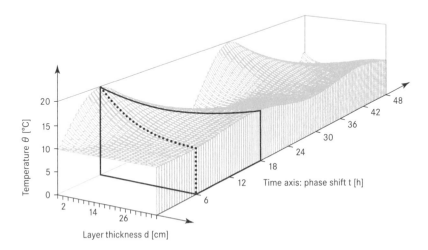

PERIODIC EXCITATION:
B PENETRATION DEPTH σ [m]

Measures how far a temperature variation (heat wave) reaches into material layers.

Proportional to the square root of the thermal conductance a:

σ [m] $\approx \sqrt{a}$

therefore:

$$\sigma = \sqrt{\frac{T \cdot \lambda}{\pi \cdot c \cdot \rho}} = \sqrt{\frac{T}{\pi}} \cdot \sqrt{a}$$

Penetration depth σ_{24} for T = 1 day:
$\sigma_{24} = 165.8 \cdot \sqrt{a}$ [m]

T = 86,400 s = 24 h

Penetration depth σ_y for T = 1 year:
$\sigma_y = 3,168.3 \cdot \sqrt{a}$ [m]

T = 31.5 · 10^6 s

Decrease in temperature variation
$\Delta\theta_{(x)} = \Delta\theta_0 \cdot e^{-\frac{x}{\sigma}}$

Decrease at layer thickness d:
d = σ: 36.7% (e^{-1}) of the amplitude
d = 2σ: 13.5% (e^{-2}) of the amplitude
d = 3σ: 5.0% (e^{-3}) of the amplitude

i.e. after a material layer of thickness d = 3σ, the variation is nearly imperceptible.

AMOUNT OF EXCHANGED ENERGY Q_T [J/m²]

Measure of the amount of energy entering and leaving the material per period T and per m² = heat storage charge and discharge (layer of infinite thickness):

$$Q_T = 2 \cdot \sqrt{\frac{T}{2\pi} \cdot \rho \cdot c \cdot \lambda} \cdot \Delta\theta = 2 \cdot \sqrt{\frac{T}{2\pi}} \cdot b \cdot \Delta\theta$$

Amount of energy exchanged Q_{24}
for T = 1 day:
$Q_{24} = 2 \cdot 117.3 \cdot b \cdot \Delta\theta$

Amount of energy exchanged Q_y
for T = 1 year:
$Q_y = 2 \cdot 2,240.3 \cdot b \cdot \Delta\theta$

Example for reinforced concrete
Day temperature amplitude $\Delta\theta$ = 6K
Thermal conductance a = 68 · 10^{-8} [m²s]
Thermal admittance b = 2.18 [kJ/m² · K · $s^{\frac{1}{2}}$]

Penetration depth daily variation
$\sigma_{24} = 165.8 \cdot \sqrt{a} = 165.8 \cdot \sqrt{68 \cdot 10^{-8}} = 0.136$ m

Penetration depth yearly variation
$\sigma_y = 3,168.3 \cdot \sqrt{a} = 3,168.3 \cdot \sqrt{68 \cdot 10^{-8}} = 2.61$ m

Amount of heat exchange for day Q_{24}
$Q_{24} = 2 \cdot 117.3 \cdot 2.18 \cdot 6 = 6,137.1$ kJ/m² $\cong 3.1$ MJ/m²

table of material values: see annex

B PENETRATION DEPTH σ [m] – DECREASE WITH MATERIAL DEPTH d

Temperature profile of a heat wave into a wall (e.g. concrete)

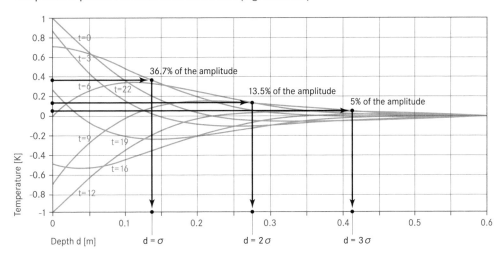

B PENETRATION DEPTH σ [m]

of different materials at common construction thicknesses

Material	Thermal conductance a	Common thickness d	Penetration depth σ [m]	
	a [10⁻⁸m²/s]	d [m]	T [s] = 1 year	T [s] = 1 day
			31,536,000 s	86,400 s
Wood (spruce)	14	0.05	1.18	0.062
Pavatherm	10	0.05	1.00	0.052
Brick	44	0.30	2.10	0.110
Insulating brick (Optitherm)	20	0.475	1.42	0.074
Lime brick	62	0.15	2.50	0.131
Reinforced concrete	68	0.20	2.61	0.137
Aerated concrete	26	0.50	1.62	0.065
Polystyrene	167	0.12	4.09	0.214
Rockwool 80 kg/m³	83	0.12	2.89	0.151
Foam glass	44	0.12	2.10	0.110
Steel	1,528		12.39	0.648
Aluminium	8,230		28.74	1.504

PERIODIC EXCITATION:
C **DYNAMIC HEAT STORAGE CAPACITY**
C [J/m²K]
Measure of the capability of thermal absorption = heat storage capacity [J/m²K], referring to the area in m² with thickness d

1. If layer thickness less than

$$d \leq \frac{1}{\sqrt{2}} \cdot \sigma$$

Heat storage capacity C [J/m²K]
→ dependent on layer thickness d
$C = c \cdot \rho \cdot d$ [J/m²K]

where:
c: Specific heat capacity [kJ/kgK]
ρ: Specific density [kg/m³]
$c \cdot \rho$: Specific volumetric heat capacity [kJ/m³K]
d: Layer thickness [m]

2. If layer thickness greater than

$$d \geq \frac{1}{\sqrt{2}} \cdot \sigma$$

Heat storage capacity C [J/m²K]
→ independent of layer thickness d

$$C = \sqrt{\frac{T}{2\pi}} \cdot b \ [J/m^2K]$$

where:
T: Time [s]
b: Specific thermal admittance [kJ/m²Ks$^{1-2}$]

C DYNAMIC HEAT STORAGE CAPACITY C [J/m²K]

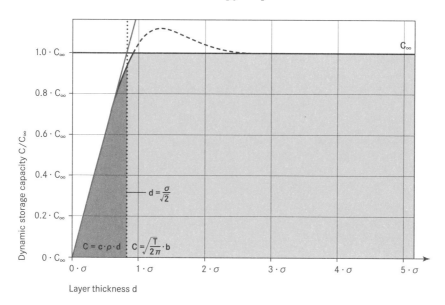

Layer thickness d

$\cdots\cdots$ $d = \dfrac{\sigma}{\sqrt{2}}$

▬▬▬   Thin layer

▬▬▬   Thick layer

D PRE-RESISTANCE R_{Pr} [m² K/W]
Reduction of the effective heat storage capacity C

An additional layer, such as a suspended metal ceiling or a carpet, between the heat storage capacity C and the room, reduces the effective heat storage capacity of e.g. a slab:
→ Pre-resistance R_{Pr}

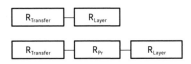

For a suspended ceiling sC the pre-resistance R_{Pr} is given by:

$R_{Pr} = R_{sC} + R_{hollow\ space}$

If hollow space larger than 10 cm:
$R_{hollow\ space} = 0.20\ m^2K/W$

$$\beta_1 = \frac{R_{Transfer}}{R_{Layer}}$$

$$\beta_2 = \frac{R_{Pr}}{R_{Layer}}$$

Capacity reduction by a pre-resistance R_{Pr} – procedure

1. Determine complete pre-resistance R_{Pr}

2. Then compute $\beta_2 = \dfrac{R_{Pr}}{R_{Layer}}$

3. Read reduction factor $C_{with} / C_{without}$ from the graph

Examples

Suspended metal ceiling with rockwool layer
→ metal sheet negligible
Rockwool layer:
d = 5 cm
λ = 0.04 W/mK
Hollow space:
d = 20 cm
Concrete slab:
thickness 20 cm → relevant for computation:
d = 10 cm
λ = 1.8 W/mK

1. Total resistance (metal sheet negligible)
$$R_{Pr} = \frac{d}{\lambda} + 0.2 = \frac{0.05}{0.04} + 0.2 = 1.45\ m^2K/W$$

2. $R_{Layer} \geq \dfrac{d}{\lambda} \geq \dfrac{0.1}{1.8} = 0.05$

$$\beta_2 = \frac{R_{Pr}}{R_{Layer}} = \frac{1.45}{0.05} = 29$$

3. From the graph: curve for concrete
$\beta_1 = 3 : C_{with} / C_{without} = 0.12$

The dynamic storage capacity is thus reduced to 12%.

Suspended metal ceiling without rockwool layer
→ metal sheet negligible
Hollow space:
d = 20 cm
Concrete slab:
thickness 20 cm → relevant for computation:
d = 10 cm
λ = 1.8 W/mK

1. Pre-resistance $R_{hollow\ space} = 0.2\ m^2K/W$

2. $\beta_2 = \dfrac{R_{Pr}}{R_{Layer}} = \dfrac{0.2}{0.05} = 4$

3. From the graph:
$C_{with} / C_{without} = 0.5$, thus a reduction to 50%.

D PRE-RESISTANCE R_{Pr} [m² K/W]
Reduction of the effective heat storage capacity C

Reduction by pre-resistance

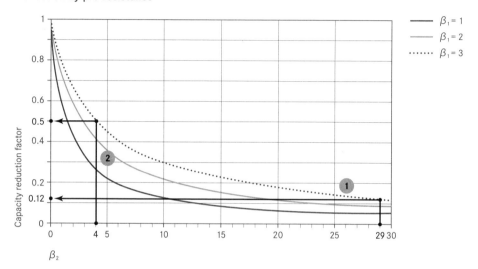

Construction above suspended ceilings:
β_1 = 1: for wooden slabs
β_1 = 2: for mixed constructions
β_1 = 3: for concrete slabs

Examples:
1 Suspended metal ceiling with rockwool layer
2 Suspended metal ceiling without rockwool layer

APERIODIC EXCITATION:
E TIME CONSTANT τ [s]

The time constant τ is the measure for the reaction time of a building component due to a sudden change in weather conditions: thunderstorm etc.

"Inertia" or "thermal memory"

Time constant τ for a single layer

$$\tau = \frac{d^2}{a \cdot \mu_1^2} \ [s]$$

$0 \le \mu_1 \le \dfrac{\pi}{2}$ in first approximation $\mu_1 \cong 1$

with
R: resistance
R_e: transitionresistance
C: heat storage capacity

and

$$\beta = \frac{R_e}{R} :$$

β =	0	0.05	0.5	1	3	10	
μ_1 =	1.57	1.48	1.1	0.86	0.55	0.3	$\dfrac{1}{\sqrt{\beta}}$

$$\tau \cong \frac{d^2}{a} = R \cdot C \ [s]$$

F REACTION TO SUDDEN CHANGE

Adaptation to changed conditions with
τ small: rapid
τ large: slow

The smaller the thermal conductance a, the greater the thickness d
→ the larger the time constant τ of a layer

Rough approximation of the time constant τ for multilayer structures

$\tau = R \cdot C$
$R = \Sigma \ (d_i / \lambda_i)$, $C = \Sigma \ (d_i \cdot c_i \cdot \rho_i)$

After 3τ, the layer is nearly in equilibrium with its environment, the impact of the weather change is barely perceptible (5%).
see "penetration depth" pages 48–49

The effect of the inertia of a building element is always symmetrical: a massive component takes a long time to switch from a cold to a warm state, and vice versa. Therefore no energy gain can be achieved.

E TIME CONSTANT τ [s]

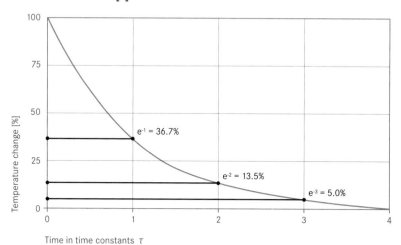

$e^{-1} = 36.7\%$

$e^{-2} = 13.5\%$

$e^{-3} = 5.0\%$

Temperature change [%]

Time in time constants τ

F REACTION TO SUDDEN CHANGE
Comparison of insulating brick – insulated metal panel

Material	Insulating brick	Metal panel: aluminum/ rockwool/steel
Material properties		
Thickness d [m]	0.475	0.003 0.12 0.002
Thermal conductivity λ [W/m²K]	0.2	220 0.04 55
Specific heat capacity c [J/kgK]	900	900 600 500
Density ρ [kg/m³]	1,100	2,700 100 7,850
Thermal resistance R = Σd/λ [m²K/W]	2.375	3.0
Heat capacity C = Σd · c · ρ [kJ/m²K] per area and temperature	470.25	22.34
Time constant τ = R · C [s]	1,116,844 s = 310 h = 12.9 d	67,020 s = 18.6 h = 0.8 d
Reaction time	Days	Hours

ENERGY TRANSFER THROUGH THE OPAQUE BUILDING ENVELOPE

A STATIONARY EFFECTS: TEMPERATURE AND IRRADIATION

Temperature difference $\Delta\theta$: constant $\neq 0$
Heat flux q: constant $\neq 0$
Thermal state: balanced flow, equilibrium

**MEAN VALUE OF
HEAT FLUX DENSITY $\bar{q}$ [W]**

$$\bar{q} = \left[(\theta_{ai} - \theta_e) - \frac{a \cdot \bar{I}}{h_e} \right] \cdot U \text{ [W]}$$

Direction of flux independent of U-value

Direction of heat flux – definition:
$\bar{q} > 0$, positive
from inside to outside

$$\bar{q} > 0 : (\theta_{ai} - \theta_e) > \frac{a \cdot \bar{I}}{h_e}$$

$\bar{q} < 0$, negative
from outside to inside

$$\bar{q} < 0 : (\theta_{ai} - \theta_e) < \frac{a \cdot \bar{I}}{h_e}$$

where:
I: Solar radiation intensity [W/m^{2}K]
a: Absorption of external surface [–]
h_e: External heat transfer coefficient [W/m^{2}K]
h_i: Internal heat transfer coefficient [W/m^{2}K]
θ_e: External temperature [°C]
θ_{ai}: Internal ambient temperature [°C]

A STATIONARY EFFECT OF TEMPERATURE AND IRRADIATION
schema: heat flow divider for the absorbed radiation

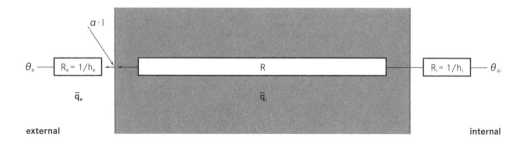

external   internal

ABSORPTION a OF DIFFERENT MATERIALS

Silver paint, with aluminium particles	0.10		Concrete, mortar	approx. 0.60
White varnish	0.21		Asphalt, old	0.88
White paint	0.26		Roofing felt green, brown	0.85–0.90
Aluminium-bronze	0.54		Fibre cement plates, new	0.42
Brown, green paint	0.79		Fibre cement plates, one year old	0.71
Black paint	0.94		Slate plates	0.90
Polished copper sheet	0.18		Wood new or grey, weathered	0.35
Matt copper sheet	0.64		Roof tiles, raw	0.43
Raw aluminium	0.63		Brickwork, raw	0.56
New zinc sheet	0.64		White ceramic tiles	0.18
Old lead sheet	0.79			
Electroplated iron, dirty	0.94			

**NON-STATIONARY EFFECTS:
TEMPERATURE TRANSMITTANCE TT
RADIATION BASED HEAT TRANSMIT-
TANCE RHT**

Difference in temperature $\Delta\theta$: variable
Heat flux q: variable

**Simple computation of two "ideal"
extreme cases: isotherm and adiabatic**
They do not exist in reality, but different
types of construction can be characterized
as follows:

**I ISOTHERMAL = MASSIVE
CONSTRUCTION**
Interior space has very good storage capacity

Absorbtion of all incoming heat in the massive
building structure of the interior space or by
compensation through the HVAC equipment

Heat flux variation maximum, ~ Δq

**No temperature variation inside, $\Delta\theta_i = 0$
(isotherm)**
→ Relevant to design of HVAC equipment

II ADIABATIC = LIGHTWEIGHT STRUCTURE
Almost no storage capacity in the interior space,
lightweight structure or internal insulation

Accumulation of all incoming heat fluxes

No heat flux to the interior space, $\Delta q_i = 0$

Temperature variation maximum, ~ $\Delta\theta$
→ relevant to estimating comfort, worst case
scenario

TEMPERATURE TRANSMITTANCE TT
Effect of external temperature variation $\Delta\theta_e$

TT I isothermal	TT II adiabatic
$TT\ I = \dfrac{\Delta q_i}{\Delta\theta_e}\left[\dfrac{W}{m^2 K}\right]$	$TT\ II = \dfrac{\Delta\theta_{ai}}{\Delta\theta_e}$ [–] (no dimension)
"Dynamic U-value"	Temperature amplitude attenuation $v_T = \dfrac{1}{TT\ II}$

RADIATION BASED HEAT TRANSMITTANCE RHT
Effect of an irradiation variation $a\cdot\Delta I$

RHT I isothermal	RHT II adiabatic
$RHT\ I = \dfrac{\Delta q_i}{a\cdot\Delta I}$ [–] (no dimension)	$RHT\ II = \dfrac{\Delta\theta_{ai}}{a\cdot\Delta I}\left[\dfrac{m^2 K}{W}\right]$
Flux amplitude attenutaion $v_s = \dfrac{1}{RHT\ I}$	"Dynamic heat resistance"

The values TT I, TT II, RHT I and RHT II of multilayer constructions are computed using complex matrices.
see tables in the annex

www.pinpoint-online.ch

TOTAL BALANCE OF OPAQUE BUILDING ELEMENTS

The relevant climatic components of the environment for the computation of the total balance are
solar radiation, external and internal temperature

Computation of the total balance:
Addition of the stationary and non-stationary
effects

Stationary → mean values

Non-stationary → effect of variations

I Isothermal

Maximum and minimum heat flux density

$$(q_i)_{max,min} = \left[(\bar{\theta}_{ai} - \bar{\theta}_e) - \frac{a \cdot \bar{I}}{h_e} \right] \cdot U \pm \text{TT I} \cdot \Delta\theta_e \pm \text{RHT I} \cdot a \cdot \Delta I \quad [\text{W/m}^2]$$

(stationary — non-stationary, above the bracket)

dependent on U-value

II Adiabatic

Maximum and minimum values for room temperature

$$(\theta_{ai})_{max,min} = \bar{\theta}_e + \frac{a \cdot \bar{I}}{h_e} \pm \text{TT II} \cdot \Delta\theta_e \pm \text{RHT II} \cdot a \cdot \Delta I \quad [\text{K}]$$

(stationary — non-stationary, above)

independent of U-value

Massive construction

The transmittance values for most massive constructions are very small.
Combination of massive structures with very low U-values: The non-stationary transmittance of irradiation and temperature to the interior space is negligible.
Phase shift: Because of the very low level of transmittance, the discussion of phase shifts is no longer necessary.

Lightweight construction

The transmittance factors are much larger.
Combination of lightweight construction with very low U-values: The transmittance effect of irradiation and external temperature through large, opaque elements can still be problematic, in spite of the low U-values.
Phase shift: The phase shifts remain relatively small. The use of layers with small penetration depths and ventilated constructions help significantly in improving the performance of lightweight constructions.

STRATEGY FOR OPAQUE BUILDING ELEMENTS

With regard to the dynamic penetration of irradiation and external temperature:

1. Determine
Daily mean value of temperature $\bar{\theta}_e$
Daily temperature amplitude $\Delta\theta_e$

2. Determine
Mean value of daily irradiation $\bar{I}$
Daily amplitude of irradiation (table): ΔI

3. Obtain from table
Temperature transmittance TT I and TT II
Radiation based heat transmittance RHT I and RHT II
see annex

4. Calculate the maximum heat fluxes
to (>0) and from (<0) the room:

$$(q_i)_{max,min} = \left[(\bar{\theta}_{ai} - \bar{\theta}_e) - \frac{a \cdot \bar{I}}{h_e}\right] \cdot U \pm TT\,I \cdot \Delta\theta_e \pm RHT\,I \cdot a \cdot \Delta I$$

relevant to the design of HVAC equipment: compensation of maximum heat fluxes

$\rightarrow$ Peak power need for heating and cooling

5. Calculate the maximum temperatures:

$$(\theta_{ai})_{max,min} = \bar{\theta}_e + \frac{a \cdot \bar{I}}{h_e} \pm TT\,II \cdot \Delta\theta_e \pm RHT\,II \cdot a \cdot \Delta I$$

relevant to comfort: maximum and minimum temperatures to be expected

see example on pages 64–67

COMPARISON OF STRUCTURES – EXAMPLE

A lime brick wall and a wood stud construction
with identical U-values and absorption a are
compared under the same impact conditions:

U-value = 0.3 W/m²K
Absorption a = 0.5
Internal temperature θ_i = 22 °C (isotherm)
External heat transfer coefficient h_e = 10 W/m²

LIME BRICK WALL, EXTERNALLY INSULATED
TT I = 0.0757; TT II = 0.014; RHT I = 0.0076; RHT II = 0.0015
see annex

Summer

I Isothermal

$(q_i)_{max,min} = \left[(22 - 22) - \dfrac{0.5 \cdot 243}{10}\right] \cdot 0.3 \pm 0.0757 \cdot 10 \pm 0.0076 \cdot 0.5 \cdot 322 = -3.65 \pm 0.76 \pm 1.22$

i.e. the variation range is $-5.63 \leq q_i \leq -1.67$ W/m²
$q_i < 0$; in this case the heat flux is always inwards

II Adiabatic

$(\theta_{ai})_{max,min} = 22 + \dfrac{0.5 \cdot 243}{10} \pm 0.0145 \cdot 10 \pm 0.0015 \cdot 0.5 \cdot 322 = 34.2 \pm 0.145 \pm 0.242 = 34.2 \pm 0.386$ °C

i.e. the variation range is $33.8 °C \leq \theta_{ai} \leq 34.5 °C$

Winter

I Isothermal

$(q_i)_{max,min} = \left[(27) - \dfrac{0.5 \cdot 21.8}{10}\right] \cdot 0.3 \pm 0.0757 \cdot 5 \pm 0.0076 \cdot 0.5 \cdot 39.1 = 7.77 \pm 0.53$ W/m²

i.e. the variation range is $7.24 \leq q_i \leq 8.3$ W/m²
$q_i > 0$; in this case the heat flux is always outwards

II Adiabatic

$(\theta_{ai})_{max,min} = -5 + \dfrac{0.5 \cdot 21.8}{10} \pm 0.0145 \cdot 5 \pm 0.0015 \cdot 0.5 \cdot 39.1 = -3.91 \pm 0.10$ °C

i.e. the variation range is $4.01 °C \leq \theta_{ai} \leq -3.81 °C$

Climate in summer, e.g.
Mean value external temperature: $\bar{\theta}_e = 22\ °C$
Amplitude of temperature: $\Delta\theta_e = 10\ K$
Maximum irradiation intensity: $I_{max} = 600\ W/m^2$
Mean value of irradiation $(a_0/2)$: $\bar{I} = 243\ W/m^2$
Irradiation amplitude (a_1): $\Delta I = 322\ W/m^2$

Climate in winter, e.g.
Mean value external temperature: $\bar{\theta}_e = -5\ °C$
Amplitude of temperature: $\Delta\theta_e = 5\ K$
Maximum irradiation intensity: $I_{max} = 100\ W/m^2$
Mean value of irradiation $(a_0/2)$: $\bar{I} = 21.8\ W/m^2$
Irradiation amplitude (a_1): $\Delta I = 39.1\ W/m^2$

WOOD FRAME STRUCTURE
TT I = 0.2503; TT II = 0.153; RHT I = 0.025; RHT II = 0.0153
see annex

Summer

I Isothermal
$(q_i)_{max,min} = \left[(22-22) - \dfrac{0.5 \cdot 243}{10}\right] \cdot 0.3 \pm 0.2503 \cdot 10 \pm 0.025 \cdot 0.5 \cdot 322 = -3.65 \pm 6.53\ W/m^2$ i.e. the variation range is $-10.2 \le q_i \le 2.9\ W/m^2$ $q_i < 0$, as well as $q_i > 0$; in this case the heat flux is inwards and outwards, respectively

II Adiabatic
$(\theta_{ai})_{max,min} = 22 + \dfrac{0.5 \cdot 243}{10} \pm 0.0153 \cdot 10 \pm 0.0153 \cdot 0.5 \cdot 322 = 34.15 \pm 4\ °C$ i.e. the variation range is $30.15\ °C \le \theta_{ai} \le 38.15\ °C$

Winter

I Isothermal
$(q_i)_{max,min} = \left[(27) - \dfrac{0.5 \cdot 21.8}{10}\right] \cdot 0.3 \pm 0.2503 \cdot 5 \pm 0.025 \cdot 0.5 \cdot 39.1 = 7.77 \pm 1.74\ W/m^2$ i.e. The variation range is $6.03 \le q_i \le 9.51\ W/m^2$ $q_i > 0$; in this case the heat flux is always outwards

II Adiabatic
$(\theta_{ai})_{max,min} = -5 + \dfrac{0.5 \cdot 21.8}{10} \pm 0.153 \cdot 5 \pm 0.0153 \cdot 0.5 \cdot 39.1 = -3.91 \pm 1.06\ °C$ i.e. the variation range is $-4.97\ °C \le \theta_{ai} \le -2.85\ °C$

EXTERNAL INSULATION

I Isothermal

Maximum heat flux TT I: 0.0757 [W/m²K]; RHT I: 0.0076 [m²K/W]	Summer	Winter
Mean value	$q_i \leq -3.65$ W/m²	$q_i \leq 7.77$ W/m²
Amplitude	$\Delta q_i = \pm 1.98$ W/m²	$\Delta q_i = \pm 0.53$ W/m²
Range of variation	$-5.63 \leq q_i \leq -1.67$ W/m²	$7.24 \leq q_i \leq 8.3$ W/m²
Direction of heat flux	$q_i < 0$ inwards	$q_i > 0$ outwards

II Adiabatic

Maximum temperature variations TT II: 0.0145 [–]; RHT II: 0.0015 [m²K/W]	Summer	Winter
Mean value	$\theta_i = 34.2$ °C	$\theta_i = -3.9$ °C
Amplitude	$\Delta \theta_i = \pm 0.39$ °C	$\Delta \theta_i = \pm 0.1$ °C
Range of variation	33.8 °C $\leq \theta_i \leq 34.5$ °C	-4 °C $\leq \theta_i \leq 3.81$ °C

WOOD FRAME CONSTRUCTION

I Isothermal

Maximum heat flux TT I: 0.2503 [W/m²K]; RHT I: 0.0250 [m²K/W]	Summer	Winter
Mean value	$q_i \leq -3.65$ W/m²	$q_i \leq 7.77$ W/m²
Amplitude	$\Delta q_i = \pm 6.53$ W/m²	$\Delta q_i = \pm 1.74$ W/m²
Range of variation	$-10.2 \leq q_i \leq 2.9$ W/m²	$6.03 \leq q_i \leq 9.51$ W/m²
Direction of heat flux	$q_i < 0$ inwards $q_i > 0$ outwards	$q_i > 0$ outwards

II Adiabatic

Maximum temperature variations TT II: 0.1530 [–]; RHT II: 0.0153 [m²K/W]	Summer	Winter
Mean value	$\theta_i = 34.2$ °C	$\theta_i = -3.9$ °C
Amplitude	$\Delta\theta_i = \pm 4.0$ °C	$\Delta\theta_i = \pm 1.06$ °C
Range of variation	30.2 °C $\leq \theta_i \leq$ 38.2 °C	-4.95 °C $\leq \theta_i \leq$ -2.85 °C

Result
1. The mean values of the heat flux are determining. The effect of the variations is small.
2. Light structures show greater variation.

TRANSPARENT ELEMENTS

A ENERGY TRANSMISSION

by the glazing, incident radiation I_o is divided
into reflection, absorption and transmission.

RADIATION TRANSMISSION τ_E

$$\tau_E = \frac{I}{I_0} \ [-] \ \text{[no dimension]}$$

Part of the incident radiation I_o falls directly
into the room as radiation

Transmission I consists of:
visible light
UV ultraviolet and IR infrared radiation

SECONDARY HEAT RELEASE QUOTIENT q_i

$$q_i = \frac{I_{qi}}{I_0} \ [-] \ \text{[no dimension]}$$

Part of incident radiation I_0 that is absorbed
by the glazing and partially transferred to the
room by the warm inner surface

SECONDARY HEAT RELEASE I_{qi}
to interior rooms by
infrared radiation
convection

Strong absorption a by the glazing leads to
a high secondary heat release I_q:
increased static pressure in the glazing and
stress on the sealings, reducing the life of the
glazing compound.
Surface temperatures up to 40 °C in summer
are possible:
→ discomfort near the glazing

TOTAL SOLAR ENERGY TRANSMISSION g

$$g = \frac{I + I_{qi}}{I_0} = \tau_E + q_i \ [-] \ \text{[no dimension]}$$

total energy ratio of the incident radiation I_o
that arrives in a room via a radiation permeable
layer

Sum of radiation transmission τ_E and
secondary heat release quotient q_i

U_g-VALUE
$U_g = 1.5 \rightarrow 0.4 \ [W/m^2K]$

The greater the proportion of the glazing in
the building envelope and the greater the
height of the glazing itself, the lower should
be the U_g-value selected, both for energy
saving and comfort.
The U_g-values influence the surface temperature of the glazing compound inside and thus
the boundary layer and the cold air draught.
see comfort conditions

DAYLIGHT TRANSMISSION τ_v
$\tau_v \ [-] \ \text{[no dimension]}$

Indicates the ratio of visible light that arrives in
the room, wavelengths from 380 nm to 780 nm
– daylight sensitivity of the eye

Daylight transmission τ_v should never be lower
than 20% because of the daylight quality in the
interior :
→ sun glass effect
see chapter daylighting

A ENERGY TRANSMISSION

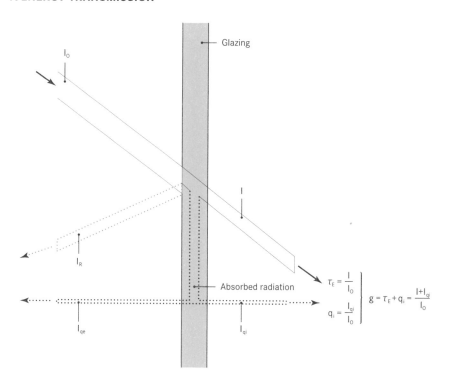

$$\tau_E = \frac{I}{I_0}$$

$$q_i = \frac{I_{qi}}{I_0}$$

$$g = \tau_E + q_i = \frac{I + I_{qi}}{I_0}$$

I_0: Total incident radiation energy (ultraviolet; visible light; infrared)
I_R: Reflected radiation
I_{qe}: Secondary heat release external
I_{qi}: Secondary heat release internal
q_i: Secondary heat release quotient
I: Transmitted radiation intensity
τ_E: Radiation transmission
g: Total energy transmission

B SPECTRAL SELECTIVITY S

$$S = \frac{\tau_V}{g} \ [-] \ \text{[no dimension]}$$

Quotient of daylight transmission τ_V and total solar energy transmission g.
High selectivity, $S > 1$,
→ preference of daylight against the non-visible range of the radiation
→ reduces the cooling load

COLOUR RENDITION INDEX R_a

R_a [-] [no dimension]

Quantifies the degree of colour distortion of the light by the glazing.

Transmission depends on the wavelength
→ influences the colour rendition
→ if $R_a > 0.9$: the colour changes are usually not detectable by the human eye.

B SPECTRAL SELECTIVITY S

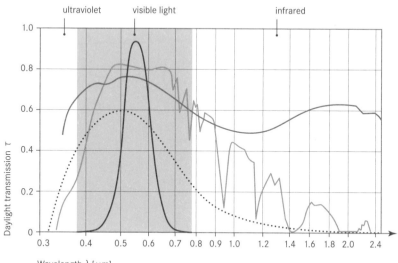

————— Eye ⎱ relative units
————— Sun ⎰

————— Triple glazing: not selective

········· Coated low-e glazing: selective

CHARACTERISTIC VALUES OF GLAZING – EXAMPLES

Glazing	Thickness	Daylight transmission	Total energy transmission
Name	mm	τ_v	g
Single glazing	4–8	0.90	0.86
Double glazing	18–22	0.82	0.77
Triple glazing	30–32	0.76	0.69
Silverstar V, double	20	0.74	0.57
Silverstar V, triple	33	0.62	0.42
Silverstar W, double	24	0.79	0.64
Silverstar W, triple	33	0.69	0.52
Silverstar Selekt, double	20	0.73	0.41
Silverstar Selekt, triple	29	0.60	0.35
Combi Neutral 70/40	24	0.70	0.40
Antelio, double	26	0.39	0.34
Antelio Climaplus, double	26	0.39	0.34
Parsol Climaplus, double	26	0.62	0.37
Cool-Lite, double	26	0.43	0.39
Climasol 66/38	22	0.66	0.38
Parelio 24+WS	24	0.62	0.43
Insulight Sun Bril 66/33	28	0.66	0.33
Insulight Sun Silb 36/22	28	0.36	0.22
Insulight Sun Silb 14/17	28	0.15	0.17
Insulight Therm 2x4OFX	16	0.76	0.61
Insulight Therm 3x4OFA	36	0.64	0.45
Insulight Therm 3x4OFX	28	0.64	0.45
Insulight Suncool Blue	36	0.24	0.21
Insulight Suncool Silver	34	0.08	0.11
Unisun Silver 19/17	28	0.19	0.19
Unisun Silver 9/9	28	0.09	0.11
Unisun Green 22/16	28	0.22	0.18
Unisun Green 16/13	28	0.16	0.15

see manufacturers' indications

Radiation transmission	Secondary heat release quotient	Spectral selectivity	U_g-value
τ_E	q_i	S	U_g
0.82	0.04	1.04	> 5
0.73	0.04	1.07	2.95
0.63	0.06	1.09	2.04
0.47	0.10	1.30	1.00
0.33	0.09	1.48	0.50
0.54	0.10	1.23	1.10
0.42	0.10	1.33	0.70
0.38	0.03	1.78	0.90
0.27	0.08	1.71	0.60
0.35	0.05	1.75	1.30
–	–	1.15	1.20
–	–	1.15	1.10
–	–	1.68	1.20
–	–	1.10	1.40
–	–	1.74	1.30
0.34	0.09	1.45	1.50
–	–	2.00	1.00
–	–	1.64	1.10
–	–	0.82	1.10
–	–	1.25	0.90
–	–	1.42	0.70
–	–	1.42	0.40
–	–	–	1.70
–	–	–	1.60
–	–	–	1.20
–	–	–	1.20
–	–	–	1.20
–	–	–	1.20

C SUN SHADING
Variable external sun shading is most effective:
→ it blocks both direct and diffuse radiation

D Reduction factor for irradiation
approximately for sun shading
external sun shade: 0.2
internal sun shade: 0.5

The better the glazing, i.e. the lower its
U_g-value, the smaller the reduction factor of
internal sun shading

Principle of construction
→ Sun shading on the facade as far outside as
possible
→ glazing with low U_g-value as far inside as
possible

If internal sun shading is used, it should be as
reflective as possible

C SUN SHADING

Sun shading	Variable	Fixed
External	Louvre blinds (slats) Roll shutters Awnings Textile screens	Porch, balcony, brises-soleil etc.
In the window	Roller blind Foils Electrochromic layers	Anti-sun glass Fixed lamellae
Internal	Curtains Venetian blinds	

D Reduction factor for irradiation

Glazing and measure [1]		τ_V	τ_E	q_i	g
2-IV	Clear glass Clear glass + external lamellae, bright Clear glass + internal lamellae, bright	0.81 0.20–0.40 0.30–0.50	0.70 0.12 0.26	0.05 0.03 0.19	0.75 0.15 0.45
2-IV-IR	Low-e glazing Low-e glazing + external lamellae, bright Low-e glazing + internal lamellae, bright	0.75 0.10–0.30 0.20–0.40	0.45 0.08 0.20	0.17 0.04 0.27	0.62 0.12 0.47
2-IV	Reflective glass [2]	0.30–0.50	0.20	0.06	0.26
3-IV	Clear glass Clear glass + external lamellae, bright Clear glass + internal lamellae, bright	0.74 0.20–0.40 0.30–0.50	0.63 0.10 0.23	0.07 0.03 0.20	0.70 0.13 0.43
3-IV-IR-IR	Low-e glazing (at least 2 coated surfaces) [3] Low-e glazing (at least 2 coated surfaces) [4] Low-e glazing + external lamellae, bright Low-e glazing + internal lamellae, bright	0.64 0.56 0.10–0.30 0.20–0.40	0.33 0.28 0.06 0.14	0.22 0.17 0.05 0.28	0.55 0.45 0.11 0.42
3-IV	Reflection glazing [2]	0.20–0.40	0.18	0.05	0.23

[1] Request data from manufacturers for special glazings
   Combinations, obtained by multiplying the factors for different systems, are not permitted
[2] Typical values: double glazing: g = 0.30; for triple glazing: g = 0.25
[3] Sequence of the glass panes from outside to inside: clear – coated – coated
[4] Sequence of the glass panes from outside to inside: coated – clear – coated

POWER BALANCE – EXAMPLE

Balance "incoming = outgoing"

$I \cdot g = U \cdot \Delta\theta$

Estimation of the total necessary energy transmission $I = g \cdot I_o$ through a transparent element to compensate for the heat transmission loss (winter case):

Example

U-value: 1.0 W/m²K
g-value: 0.6
$\Delta\theta$: 30 K (outside -10 °C; inside +20 °C)

$$I = \frac{U}{g} \cdot \Delta\theta = \frac{1}{0.6} \cdot 30 = 50 \text{ W/m}^2$$

Energy balance

in this case positive as soon as
→ incident radiation $I \geq 50$ W/m²

This intensity of incident radiation I corresponds to a heavily clouded sky.

→ The energy balance in this case is almost always positive during the day.

SIGNIFICANCE OF THE CHARACTERISTIC VALUES – EXAMPLE
Comparison of two glazings
Incident radiation intensity I_o = 600 W/m^2
Internal heat transfer coefficient h_i = 8 W/m^{2}K

	Double glazing air filled	Low-e glazing e.g. "Silverstar W", double
U_g-value [W/m^{2}K]	2.95	1.1
g-value [–]	0.77	0.64
τ_E [–]	0.73	0.54
q_i [–]	0.04	0.1
Radiation transmission $I = \tau_E \cdot I_0$ [W/m^2]	437	324
Secondary heat release $I_q = q_i \cdot I_0$ [W/m^2]	24	60
Total energy transmission $I_{tot} = I + I_q$ [W/m^2]	461	384
Temperature difference between glass surface and ambient air $\Delta\theta_{ai} = \dfrac{I_q}{h_i}$ [K]	3.0	7.5

for glazings see page 72–73

AIR INFILTRATION

REQUIRED MINIMUM AIR CHANGE RATE
necessary for any building and its users for:

Fresh air
depending on the situation 15–30 m³/h
per person, e.g. smoker, non-smoker

Air hygiene
to provide oxygen supply
EN 12831

Limitation of pollutants
e.g. to keep CO_2 level low

A **Limitation of air humidity**
Avoiding condensation problems
SIA 180

ASSUMED MAXIMUM AIR CHANGE RATE
for the design of HVAC equipment

The energy exchange with the environment and
the corresponding maximum heating and cooling power needed is mainly determined by the
maximum assumed air change rate
SN EN 12831

EXPECTED MEAN AIR CHANGE RATE
relevant to the computation of the energy need
for heating and cooling
SIA 380/1

see stationary heat transmission:
loss factor due to air change

A Limitation of air humidity
Maximum of acceptable average interior air humidity
Determination of the minimum external air change rate

Followng day mean values must be kept:									
External air temperature θ_e in °C	+20	+15	+10	+5	0	-5	-10	-15	-20
$v_{i,max}$ in g/m^3	13.5	11.9	10.5	9.3	8.2	7.3	6.5	5.8	5.2
$p_{i,max}$ in Pa	1,823	1,605	1,418	1,255	1,114	988	880	786	703
$\varphi_{i,max}$ in % when θ_i = 20 °C	78	69	61	54	48	42	38	34	30
Dew point temperature $\theta_{i,D}$ in °C	16.0	14.1	12.2	10.3	8.6	6.8	5.1	3.5	1.9

SIA 180, 3.1.3.5

REQUIRED MINIMUM AIR CHANGE RATE $\dot{V}_{min,i}$ [m³/h]

for air hygiene and to limit humidity:

$$\dot{V}_{min,i} \geq 15 \; \frac{m^3}{h} \quad \text{per person}$$

$$\dot{V}_{min,i} = n_{min} \cdot V_i \, [m^3/h]$$

n_{min}: Minimum air change per hour [h⁻¹]
V_i: Volume of the heated room, internal dimensions [m³]
EN 12831

or:

$$\dot{V}_{min,i} \left[\frac{m^3}{h} \right] \geq \frac{G\,[g/h]}{(C_{max} - C_e)[g/m^3]}$$

$$\dot{V}_{min,i} \geq \frac{G}{v_{i,max} - v_e}$$

B Production of pollutants G in a room [g/h]

G: Moisture production in a room [g/h]

Maximum acceptable pollution concentration C_{max} [g/m³]

$v_{i,max}$: Maximum acceptable air humidity in a room [g/m³]

Pollution concentration of the external air C_e [g/m³]

v_e: Absolute humidity of the external air [g/m³]

Determination of the required minimum air change rate

Example

External temperature:
$0\,°C \rightarrow v_{i,max} \leq 8.2 \; g/m^3$

External humidity*:
$80\% \rightarrow v_e = 4.85 \times 0.8 = 3.88 \; g/m^3$
* see chapter humidity, water vapour pressure tables

Production of humidity G inside
e.g. household: G = 60–90 g/h

$$\dot{V}_{min} \geq \frac{G}{v_{i,max} - v_e}$$

$$\dot{V}_{min} \geq \frac{90}{8.2 - 3.88} = \frac{90}{4.32} \cong 20.8 \; m^3/h$$

Required minimum air change rate
Room: 60 m³

$$60 \; m^3 \rightarrow n \geq \frac{\dot{V}_{min}}{V} \cong \frac{20.8}{60} \cong 0.3/h$$

B Moisture production G in a room [g/h]
  Guideline values for typical moisture sources

Moisture source	Moisture production G [g/h]
Person, easy work	30–60
Person, household work	60–90
Person, heavy work	100–200
Cooking	400–800
Dishwasher	200–400
Shower	1,500–3,000
Bathtub	600–1,200
Open water surface (per m²)	30–50
Potted plant	7–15
Rubber plant (Ficus)	10–20

SIA 180, 3.1.3.3

B Moisture production G in a room [g/h · m²]
  Mean moisture production in a room G/A_{nfa}
  Guideline values

Moisture source	Moisture production G [g/h · m²]	Function
low	2	living low occupation, few plants offices, administration, shops, warehouses
medium	4	living dense occupation, many plants schools, meeting rooms
high	6	restaurants, kitchens, gyms, hospitals
very high	> 10	laundries, wet production processes

SIA 180, 3.1.3.4

ASSUMED MAXIMUM AIR CHANGE RATE

Air infiltration – air flow rate $\dot{V}_{inf,i}$ [m³/h]

Air flow rate $\dot{V}_{inf,i}$ based on wind and buoyancy produces pressure differences

$$\dot{V}_{inf,i} = 2 \cdot V_i \cdot n_{50} \cdot e_i \cdot \varepsilon_i \ [m^3/h]$$

V_i: Air volume of the heated rooms [m³]
n_{50}: Air change rate per hour [h⁻¹]
at 50 Pa pressure difference
e_i: Shielding coefficient [–]
ε_i: Height correction factor [–]
2: Correction factor [–]
because the n_{50}-values refer to the whole building

Air transmissivity values n_{50}

Type of building	n_{50} [h⁻¹]		
	Degree of leakiness of the building envelope		
	leakproof	moderately leaky	leaky
Single family houses	4	7	10
Other buildings	2	4	5

Shielding coefficient e [–]

Shielding class	Interior room without external wall	Room with external wall in one direction	Room with several external walls
No shielding: Buildings in windy locations, high-rise buildings	0	0.03	0.05
Moderate shielding: Freestanding buildings, surrounding trees or other buildings, suburbs	0	0.02	0.03
Good shielding: Medium-height buildings in city centres, forested areas	0	0.01	0.02

Height correction factor ε [–]
of a room for its height above ground

Height above ground	ε
0–10 m	1.0
10–20 m	1.3
20–30 m	1.4
30–40 m	1.6
40–50 m	1.7
50–60 m	1.8
60–80 m	2.0
> 80 m	2.2

EXPECTED MEAN AIR CHANGE RATE

Specific external air flow rate
v_a [m³/h·m²] for standard use
SIA 380/1, 3.5.1.9.1

$$v_a = \frac{\dot{V}}{A_E} \ [m^3/h \cdot m^2]$$

$\dot{V}$: External air flow [m³/h]
A_E: Energy-relevant floor area [m²]

Building category	Standard uses	Specific external air flow v_a [m³/h·m²]
I	Living, multifamily houses	0.7
II	Living, single family houses	0.7
III	Offices	0.7
IV	Schools	0.7
V	Shops	0.7
VI	Restaurants	1.2
VII	Meeting rooms	1.0
VIII	Hospitals	1.0
IX	Industry	0.7
X	Warehouses	0.3
XI	Gymnasiums	0.7
XII	Indoor swimming pools	0.7

These values include air change due to exhaust air installations, as in kitchens, bathrooms and toilets.

Air change rate n

$$n = \frac{v_a}{h} \ [h^{-1}]$$

h: Room height [m]

Loss factor F_{Lac} due to air change [W/K]

$$F_{Lac} = n \cdot V \frac{(c \cdot \rho)_{Air}}{3,600} \ [W/K]$$

where $(c \cdot \rho)_{Air} = 1200 \ \left[\frac{J}{m^2 \cdot K}\right]$

n: Assumed mean air change rate
V: Room volume → room geometry

$$F_{Lac} \cong \frac{n \cdot V}{3}$$

Estimation of the heat loss P [W]
by the assumed mean air change rate
$P = F_{Lac} \cdot \Delta\theta$

LIMITING AND TARGET VALUES FOR THE AIRTIGHTNESS OF THE BUILDING ENVELOPE $v_{a,4,max}$ [m³/h·m²]

$v_{a,4,max}$ [m³/h·m²]
Air change in m³/hm² at $\Delta p = 4$ Pa

Category	$v_{a,4,max}$ [m³/h·m²]	
	limiting value	target value
New buildings	0.75	0.5
Conversions, renovations	1.5	1.0

SIA 180, 3.1.4.6

$$v_{a,4} = \frac{\dot{V}_4}{A_e} \ [m^3/h \cdot m^2]$$

$\dot{V}_4$: Air flow volume at 4 Pa pressure difference in m³/h for standard conditions (101,325 Pa, 0 °C)
A_e: External surface

Buildings with mechanical ventilation equipment must meet the target values.

DESIGN PRINCIPLES

New buildngs

Fresh air supply by opening windows or comfort ventilation (MINERGY)
Rooms as airtight as possible Planning and choice of construction to allow intermediate inspections during execution Quality control: care of execution on site all joints of installations airtight sun shading boxes including crank joint airtight Silicon-sealed joining (wet) of window frame and glazing is more airtight than rubber-sealed joining (dry). Exposed to wind pressure, strong frames are tighter than light, elegant ones. Sashes should have the fittings near to the corners, top and bottom. Kitchen and toilet ventilation should have an automatic flap, open only while in use Chimneys equipped with flaps for closing Air supply for chimneys/fireplaces with facility to preheat the air

Conversions, renovations

If windows are replaced by new, airtight ones: **Improvement of U-values of the external envelope** must be examined to avoid moisture/condensation problems due to the reduced "natural" air change Check thermal bridges to avoid condensation
Supply of fresh air mechanical comfort ventilation (MINERGY) or well-directed window ventilation by opening routines → users must be informed

DYNAMIC KEY FIGURES FOR A ROOM

The thermodynamic behaviour of a room is completely determined by the following three figures:

LOSS FACTOR K [W/m²K]

$$K' = \sum_i A_i \cdot U_i + n \cdot V \cdot \frac{(c \cdot \rho)_{Air}}{3600}$$

$$\cong \sum_i A_i \cdot U_i + \frac{1}{3_i} \cdot n \cdot V \quad [W/K]$$

A_i: Area of external surfaces [m²]
U_i: U-values of external elements [W/m²K]
n: Air change rate due to air infiltration [h¹]
V: Room volume [m³]

The loss factor K, referring to the sum of external surfaces, is relevant

$$K = \frac{K'}{\sum_i A_{e_i}} \quad \left[\frac{W}{m^2K}\right]$$

RADIATION RECEIVING AREA A'$_{RR}$ [m²]

$$A'_{RR} = \sum_i A_{tr-i} \cdot g_i$$

A_{tr-i}: Area of all transparent external elements etc.
g_i: Total solar energy transmission factors of these transparent elements

MEAN RADIATION TRANSMISSIVITY G [–]

The mean radiation transmissivity G of the radiation impact area A'$_{RR}$, referring to the sum of all the external surfaces A$_e$, is relevant

$$G = \frac{A'_{RR}}{\sum_i A_{e_i}} \quad [-] \text{ mean radiation transmissivity}$$

DYNAMIC HEAT STORAGE CAPACITY C [J/m²K]

$$C' = \sum_n A_n \cdot C_n \quad \left[\frac{J}{K}\right]$$

A_n: Internal surfaces
C_n: Specific heat storage capacity of internal elements

The heat storage capacity C of a room, referring to the sum of the external surfaces A$_e$, is relevant

$$C = \frac{C'}{\sum_i A_e} \quad \left[\frac{J}{m^2K}\right]$$

The dynamic heat storage capacity C for a period of 24 h can be referred to as a very good approximation.

Only the inner layers up to the first insulation layer ($\lambda \leq 0.1$ W/mK) need be taken into account.

Relationship of the contributions of building elements to the heat storage capacity:
70% floor slabs
20% internal walls
10% external walls

TYPICAL HEAT STORAGE CAPACITY C

Basic construction types, with reference to floor area:

Construction type	Material	Heat storage capacity C $[kJ/m^2K]$
Light	All wood	150
Mixed	Concrete slabs, brick walls	600
Heavy	All concrete	900

COMBINATIONS OF THE KEY FIGURES

Relevant to the temperature evolution of a room:

LOSS FACTOR K [W/m²K]
see page 88

Relevant to the power need of heating and cooling and therefore determining the thermal energy need

GAIN FACTOR γ [K/W · m²]

$$\gamma = \frac{G}{K} = \frac{A'_{RR}}{K'} = \left[\frac{K}{W/m^2} \right]$$

→ **"solar temperature correction"**
correction of the effective external temperature caused by irradiation

TIME CONSTANT τ [s,h]

$$\tau = \frac{C}{K} = \frac{C'}{K'} = [s, h]$$

→ **thermal inertia of a room**

FREE-RUN TEMPERATURE (FRT)

Climate characteristic of a room
The free-run temperature of a room (FRT) is the development of the room temperature in time without active influence of heating or cooling installations.

The free-run temperature can be influenced by internal heat sources such as computers, lighting etc. and variable sun shading devices.

A **OPTIMIZATION OF THE FREE-RUN TEMPERATURE**
The optimal use of the incoming solar energy is realized by an optimization of
gain factor γ → radiation receiving area
and
time constant τ → pick-up capability or reactivity

Gain factor γ
→ **Radiation receiving area**
shifts the daily mean value of the FRT and influences the daily amplitude of the FRT as well.

Time constant τ
→ **Pick-up capability or reactivity**
influences the daily amplitude of the FRT alone

A OPTIMIZATION OF THE FREE-RUN TEMPERATURE
Manoeuvre the FRT to within the comfort range

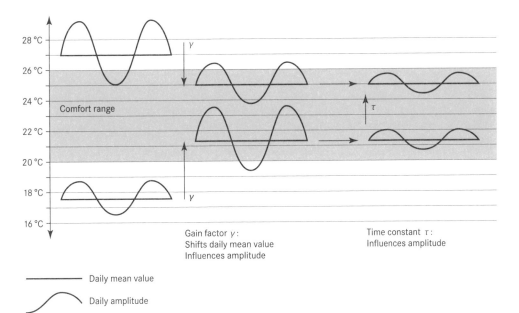

Gain factor γ:
Shifts daily mean value
Influences amplitude

Time constant τ:
Influences amplitude

———— Daily mean value

⌒ Daily amplitude

ENERGY DESIGN GUIDE (EDG)

OPTIMIZATION OF THE BUILDING ENVELOPE IN THE EARLY PLANNING

The Energy Design Guide first computes best numeric values and displays them in graphs. The curves and the relevant figures allow an interpretation that can be transferred to architectural choices such as construction type, glazing partition and glazing quality necessary for low-energy need and make a variety of architectural solutions possible.
It does not, however, quantify thermal demand.

Early energetic optimization
The EDG needs only the
loss factor K
window size/glazing quality
construction type
and is thus well suited for optimum planning at an early stage.

Optimization potential of 80–90%
can already be exploited by focusing on these most relevant factors. More complex simulation programs are thus often unnecessary.

www.pinpoint-online.ch

A CLIMATE ADAPTED OPTIMIZATION OF A ROOM
1. Loss factor K always as small as possible:
Insulation
Low-e glazing
Airtightness

2. Select the optimum combination of gain factor γ and time constant τ for the construction of a building depending on its orientation and the climate:
Energy Design Guide $\rightarrow$ climate diagrams

The best combination of gain factor γ and time constant τ results in a maximum of hours where the FRT remains within the comfort limits of 20–26 °C:
ZEH = zero-energy hours

3. The necessary glazing quality for a particular room and its glazing partition f can be chosen from the best value of the gain factor γ:
U_g-value: Heat transmission coefficient
g-value: Total solar energy transmission

see example on pages 94–97

A CLIMATE ADAPTED OPTIMIZATION OF A ROOM
Procedure for transparent elements

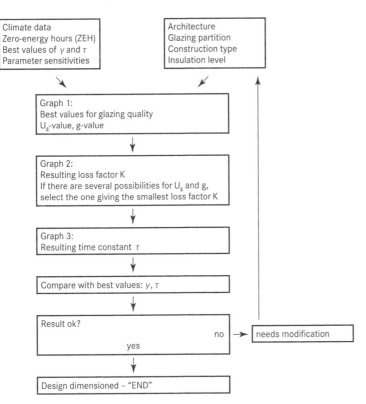

ENERGY DESIGN GUIDE – EXAMPLE

Input 1:
Location → Basel, south facade

BEST COMBINATION OF GAIN FACTOR γ AND TIME CONSTANT τ:
Highest number of zero-energy hours (ZEH)

Output 1: Climate diagram
Basel south-facing, without internal heat sources

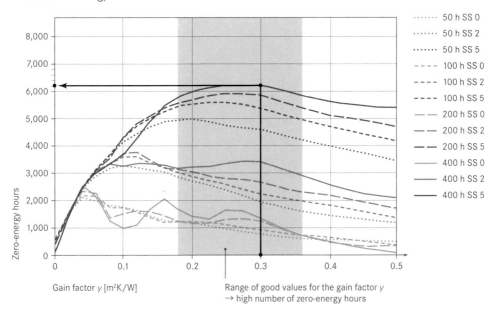

Gain factor γ [m²K/W]

Zero-energy hours

Range of good values for the gain factor γ
→ high number of zero-energy hours

Legend:
- ⋯⋯ 50 h SS 0
- ⋯⋯ 50 h SS 2
- ⋯⋯ 50 h SS 5
- − − − 100 h SS 0
- − − − 100 h SS 2
- − − − 100 h SS 5
- — — 200 h SS 0
- — — 200 h SS 2
- — — 200 h SS 5
- —— 400 h SS 0
- —— 400 h SS 2
- —— 400 h SS 5

Curves for zero-energy hours with
time constants τ: 50 h, 100 h, 200 h, 400 h
sun shading SS: SS 0 = without, SS 2 = internal, SS 5 = external

Result
The largest number of zero-energy hours is attained in Basel on the south face:
~ 6,200 ZEH per year with time constant τ = 400 h and external sun shading SS 5
(reduction of the incident radiation to ⅕)

The best value for the gain factor γ is 0.3 → possibility no. 1
A range of good values for the gain factor γ is 0.18–0.36 → possibility no. 2:
range of choice for glazing proportion f

Input 2:
Detail data for a room on the south facade

U_w: U-value wall (opaque) 0.2 W/m²k
V: Volume 108.0 m³
A_e: Total external surface 24.3 m²
A_{nfa}: Net floor area 36.0 m²
n: Air change rate due to infiltration 0.1 h⁻¹

Output 2:
Diagram 1: Best gain factor $\gamma \rightarrow$ glazing proportion f of facade

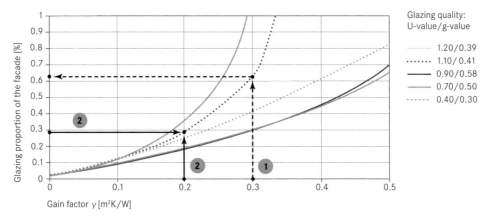

1 Possibility no. 1
   Best value of the gain factor $\gamma = 0.3$ from the climate diagram yields a glazing proportion f
   of approx. 0.62
   with a glazing quality of : U_g-value= 1.1 W/m²K; g-value = 0.41 [–]

2 Possibility no. 2
   Desired glazing proportion of the facade of about 0.28
   → the range of choice for the gain factor γ in this case also yields the best combination:
   U_g-value= 1.1 W/m²K; g-value = 0.41 [–]

Discussion:
The curves for ZEH in the climate diagram (page 95) indicate the range of possibilities that can be
exploited in the interests of architectural expression: proportion of openings/windows in the facade
with a given glazing quality in diagram 1.
The energetic consequences are illustrated in diagram 2.
The obtained results can be interpreted regarding a possible choice of construction in diagram 3.

Diagram 2: Glazing proportion f of facade → Loss factor K (or K')

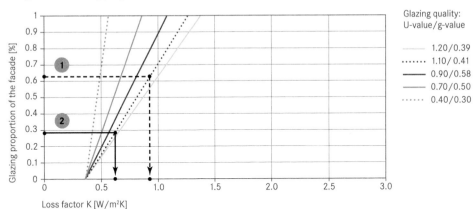

Glazing quality:
U-value/g-value

——— 1.20/0.39
••••••• 1.10/0.41
——— 0.90/0.58
——— 0.70/0.50
•••••• 0.40/0.30

1 Glazing proportion of 0.62 with the glazing quality selected results in a loss factor K ~ 0.90
2 The desired glazing proportion of 0.28 together with the same glazing quality yields a loss factor K of ~ 0.65; → energetically, this is the better solution

Diagram 3: Loss factor K → time constant τ

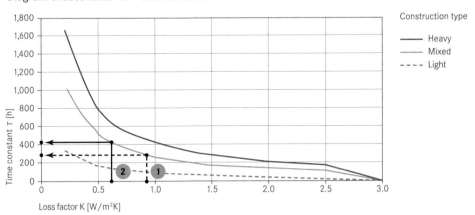

Construction type

——— Heavy
——— Mixed
– – – Light

Possibility no. 1: Time constant τ = 290 h for mixed construction: acceptable
Possibility no. 2: Time constant τ = 420 h for mixed construction: goal achieved

SOFT HVAC TECHNOLOGY

A THERMALLY ACTIVE BUILDING ELEMENTS (TAB) FOR HEATING AND COOLING

Soft HVAC technology requires the appropriate design of the building envelope to minimize thermal power needs:

Heating power density < 20–30 W/m²
Cooling power density < 40 W/m²
including internal loads of up to 75 W/m² for a limited time during a day

Under this condition, the same building element can be used for heating and cooling:
→ TAB

TAB

Plastic tubes in loops laid in the concrete slab, best at a depth of about 10 cm, but no deeper than 15 cm.
Diameter of the tubes: 18–22 mm
Distance between tubes: 30–50 cm

Heating and cooling by radiation from the ceiling permits excellent heat transfer to all surfaces in the room.

Winter

Excellent comfort because of the very small temperature differences between the ambient air of a room and its surrounding surfaces.

Summer

Excellent comfort because of the equally small temperature differences and even better because one's head is near to the cool ceiling.

Supply temperature

near to, or within the comfort range, for
Heating: 25–28 °C
Cooling: 18–21 °C

For cooling, the dew point temperature of the air must be below that of the surrounding surfaces, and below the supply temperature to avoid condensation.
see chapter moisture

Temperature difference $\Delta\theta$

between supply and return: approx. 2 K

Power P

$$P = A_T \cdot v \, (c \cdot \rho)_{H_2O} \cdot \Delta\theta \; [W]$$

A_T: Free cross section of tube in m²
v: Flow speed in m/s (0.1–1.0 m/s, normally 0.5 m/s)
$(c \cdot \rho)_{H_2O}$: Volumetric storage capacity of water
$c \cdot \rho = 4{,}182 \cdot 1{,}000 = 4.18 \cdot 10^6$ J/m³K
$\Delta\theta$: Temperature difference between supply and return 2 K

Different power densities

for corner rooms, rooms below the roof etc. can be taken into account by having two to three different supply temperatures with a switching port and a common return flow. This is possible due to the very small temperature differences.

TAB DESIGN EXAMPLE

TAB, concrete slab

Plastic tubes of 18 mm diameter
Free cross section $A_T = 2.5 \cdot 10^{-4}$ m²
Flow speed v = 0.5 m/s
Temperature difference $\Delta\theta$ = 2 K

Power P [W]

$$P = 2.54 \cdot 10^{-4} \cdot 0.5 \cdot 4.18 \cdot 10^6 \cdot 2 = 1{,}062 \; W$$

Heating

With a maximum heating power density of
< 20–30 W/m²
up to 40 m² can be heated.

Cooling

With a maximum cooling power density of
< 40 W/m²
up to 25 m² can be cooled.

A THERMALLY ACTIVE BUILDING ELEMENTS (TAB) FOR HEATING AND COOLING

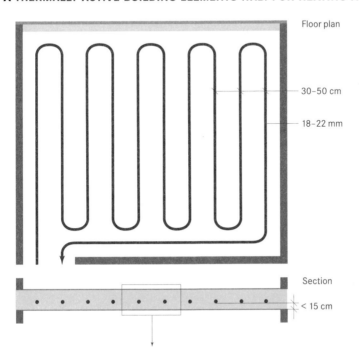

Floor plan

30–50 cm

18–22 mm

Section

< 15 cm

Temperature profile in the concrete slab (heating)

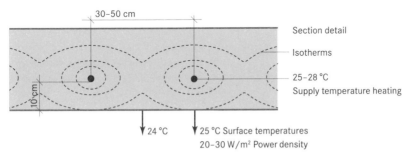

30–50 cm

Section detail

Isotherms

25–28 °C
Supply temperature heating

10 cm

24 °C   25 °C Surface temperatures
20–30 W/m² Power density

22 °C Room temperature

B COMFORT VENTILATION
Displacement principle

Fresh air is fed to the room for hygiene and comfort only. Therefore much less air is transported compared to an air conditioning system.
Need per person and hour for standard functions such as living room/office:
→ 20–30 m³/hP
i.e. air change rate n = 0.5–1.5 [h⁻¹]

No cooling function or only minor:
→ maximum approx. 10 W/m²

For passive houses, i.e. very well insulated and airtight houses, the fresh air supply can also provide cooling and heating because very little power density is needed. The inflow of warm air for heating, warmer than the ambient air, however, mixes with the room air, reducing the ventilation efficiency. In other words, one needs more fresh air inflow to attain the same cleaning effect.

Normally, no volume flow control is necessary (VAV) → on/off according to requirements.

Fresh air supply
→ Horizontal air distribution
→ Air ducts in the concrete slab, hollow floor etc.

→ Air outlet at floor level
peripheral, below windows etc.
evenly distributed

Free cross section of air outlet needed depends on air change rate and room height.
For an air change rate n ≅ 1.0 h⁻¹ and room height ≅ 3.0 m
→ approx. 3.3–5.5‰ of the floor area

Outlet flow speed:
v ≤ 0.3–0.5 m/s

Exhaust air
near ceiling, along corridor,
central collection via baths, kitchen, toilet

Vertical distribution
Ratio of cross section of air ducts needed per per m² floor area, for fresh air supply and exhaust air:

$$\frac{A_{ad}}{A} = \frac{n \cdot h}{3600 \cdot v}$$

A_{ad}: Air duct cross section [m²]
A: Floor area [m²]
n: Air change rate [h⁻¹]
h: Clear room height [m]
v: Air flow speed, 2–4 m/s

COMFORT VENTILATION
Example of dimensioning

Room height, air change rate
h = 3 m
n = 2 h⁻¹

Required space for vertical air ducts
with air speed v = 2 m/s
ratio of areas A_{ad}/A = 0.8‰

→ supply and exhaust air
1.6‰ of floor area

with air speed v = 4 m/s
ratio of areas A_{ad}/A = 0.4‰

→ supply and exhaust air
0.8‰ of floor area

In both cases, the space needed for the vertical air ducts is small because of the small air volume needed.

B COMFORT VENTILATION
   based on the displacement principle

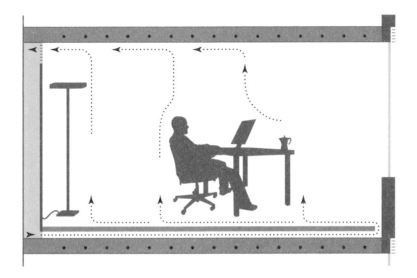

TERMS OF ENERGY MANAGEMENT

TERMS AND KEY DATA
Primary energy
Energy directly from natural resources such as hydro power, crude oil, natural gas, coal

Final energy
Energy directly available to the user: fuel oil, gas, district heating, electricity

Usable energy
Energy directly used: heat from heating, mechanical work of machines, light from the lighting

Grey or indirect energy
Accumulated need of primary energy for the production of a final product, such as a house, starting from the mining of the raw material up to renovation and final waste disposal.

Thermally enclosed floor area (TEFA)
Sum of all floor areas that are heated or air conditioned, taking into account the gross area, i.e. external dimensions including walls etc.

A Specific energy need E [MJ/m²a]
Total final energy in MJ of a building, consumed yearly and per thermally enclosed floor area in m².

Total final energy in MJ as the sum of the partial specific energy needs of:
$$E_{tot} = E_h + E_{hw} + E_{rest}$$

E_h: Specific energy need for heating
E_{hw}: Specific energy need for hot water
E_{rest}: Specific energy need for all other needs

B Key data for dimensioning the HVAC system
Determination of the applicable maximum supply temperatures based on the necessary power densities.

Goal
1. Heating power $q_H < 20$–30 W/m²
2. Cooling power $q_c < 20$–40 W/m²
3. Supply temperatures

$$\Delta\theta \cong \frac{q_H}{h_i}, \text{ with } h_i \cong 6 \text{ W/m}^2\text{K}$$

$$\Delta\theta \cong \frac{q_c}{h_i}, \text{ with } h_i \cong 8\text{–}10 \text{ W/m}^2\text{K}$$

The supply temperatures for heating and cooling should be chosen from within the comfort range

A Specific energy need E [MJ/m²a]

Switzerland	Function	Specific energy need E [MJ/m²a]
Mean values of existing buildings	Average	550
Target values of new buildings	Offices Residential (MFH) Residential (SFH)	215 358 401
"Minergy" standard values new buildings	Offices Residential (MFH/SFH)	144 151
"Minergy" standard values renovation	Offices Residential (MFH/SFH)	252 288
"Minergy-P" standard values new buildings	Offices Residential (MFH/SFH)	90 108

B Key data for the dimensioning of the HVAC systems

Typical power densities for heating

Most existing buildings	60–80 W/m²
Well-insulated buildings based on law regulations	40–60 W/m²
Buildings based on "Minergy"	15–25 W/m²
Buildings based on "Minergy-P"	10 W/m²

Power potentials of "Soft HVAC" technologies

Thermally active building elements/floor slabs: TAB

Stationary, per 24 h	up to 40 W/m²
For a limited time, e.g. a few hours	up to 75 W/m²

"Minergy-P" standard: if q_H < 10 W/m²

Displacement ventilation	8–10 W/m²

GREY ENERGY – ORDER OF MAGNITUDE
Well-insulated buildings: approximately 20% of the operating energy over 50 years
"Minergy" standard buildings: approximately 30% of the operating energy over 50 years

Well-insulated construction, heavy/massive	Grey energy
Loadbearing structure	49%
Insulation, windows, doors, sealings	17%
HVAC installations	18%
Interior work	7%
Construction site	9%
Total grey energy	100%

for 50 years' use: 100% = approx. 74 MJ/m²a

Well-insulated timber construction	Grey energy
Loadbearing structure	40%
Insulation, windows, doors, sealings	27%
HVAC installations	20%
Interior work	9%
Construction site	4%
Total grey energy	100%

for 50 years' use: 100% = approx. 59 MJ/m²a

grey energy of materials: see appendix

Conclusion

The building elements relevant to the operating energy need, such as insulation, windows and parts of the HVAC installations, consume about

→ 25% of the total grey energy, i.e. 20–30% of the operating energy over 50 years

→ only 5–7% of the total energy of a building over 50 years

Example

Given: well-insulated "traditional" building

Operating energy E	$400\ MJ/m^2a$
Grey energy, approx. 20%	$80\ MJ/m^2a$ (50 years)
Total energy consumption over 50 years	$480\ MJ/m^2a$
25% for the relevant parts	$20\ MJ/m^2a$

Measure for the reduction of the operating energy need

→ e.g. doubling investment in the relevant building elements:

Energy relevant parts	$20 + 20\ MJ/m^2a$
Grey energy, approx. 30%	$80 + 20\ MJ/m^2a$
Resulting specific energy need, approx. 70%	$200\ MJ/m^2a$
Total energy consumption over 50 years	$300\ MJ/m^2a$

i.e. additional investment in the relevant building elements of an extra $20\ MJ/m^2a$

→ reduction of the total energy need of $180\ MJ/m^2a$ over 50 years.

PRINCIPLES OF ENERGY-EFFICIENT DESIGN

THE MOST IMPORTANT ELEMENTS FOR ENERGY-EFFICIENT DESIGN

1. Building envelope
Compact design
Excellent thermal insulation
Airtightness
Variable sun shading

opaque:
U-value < 0.3, better < 0.2 W/m²K

transparent:
Low-e glazing, U_g-value < 1.2 W/m²K
depending on the size of the glazing
see pages 32–33, boundary layer flow

Climate adaptation:
thermal gain against heat storage capacity
Tool:
Energy Design Guide
Chair of Building Physics ETHZ

2. Adapted soft HVAC
Air hygiene:
Displacement ventilation
fresh air only, no recirculated air

Heating/cooling:
Radiation by thermally controlled ceilings
→ TAB
supply temperatures:
winter approximately 26 °C
summer approximately 20 °C

Supply:
via heat pump from the environment;
e.g. energy piles, ground water, air

HUMIDITY

WATER VAPOUR AND HUMIDITY

ABSOLUTE HUMIDITY v [g/m³]
Water vapour content of air in g per m^3

WATER VAPOUR PRESSURE p [Pa]
Partial pressure of the water vapour present
$p \leq p_{sat}$

A WATER VAPOUR SATURATION PRESSURE p_{sat} [Pa]
see following page
Pressure of water vapour in equilibrium with
liquid water, transition from gas to liquid and
vice versa depends on temperature, but not on
air pressure.

RELATIVE HUMIDITY φ [%]
Relationship between the actual water vapour
pressure p and the saturation pressure p_{sat} at a
given temperature

$$\varphi = \frac{p}{p_{sat}(\theta)} \cdot 100$$

DEW POINT TEMPERATURE θ_D [°C]
Temperature at which the actual water vapour
would condense, i.e. pressure corresponds to
the saturation value
$\varphi(\theta) = 100\%$ or $p = p_{sat}$

B VAPOUR PRESSURE CURVES
Show temperature dependence of the saturation
pressure p_{sat} (100%) and some partial pressures
for relative humidities of 40–80%.

B VAPOUR PRESSURE CURVES

Example

Air temperature: θ_{Air} = 20 °C

Relative humidity: φ = 40%

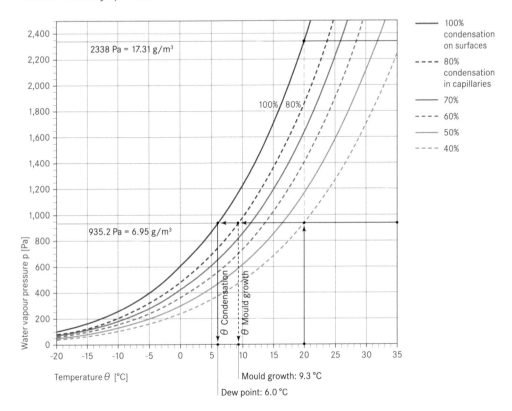

Mould growth: 9.3 °C

Dew point: 6.0 °C

A WATER VAPOUR PRESSURE TABLE p$_{sat}$ 0–35 °C

Water content of saturated air V_{sat} [g/m³]		Saturation pressure p$_{sat}$ of the water vapour [Pa = N/m²] at a temperature of [°C]									
		$^{1}/_{10}$ °C	0.0	0.1	0.2	0.3	0.4	0.5	0.6	0.7	0.8	0.9
[°C]	[g/m³]	[°C]	[Pa]	[Pa]	[Pa]	[Pa]	[Pa]	[Pa]	[Pa]	[Pa]	[Pa]	[Pa]
35	39.60	35	5,624	5,654	5,685	5,717	5,749	5,781	5,813	5,845	5,877	5,909
34	37.58	34	5,320	5,349	5,378	5,409	5,440	5,469	5,500	5,530	5,561	5,592
33	35.66	33	5,030	5,058	5,088	5,116	5,144	5,173	5,202	5,232	5,261	5,290
32	33.82	32	4,754	4,782	4,808	4,836	4,864	4,890	4,918	4,946	4,974	5,002
31	32.07	31	4,493	4,518	4,544	4,570	4,596	4,622	4,648	4,673	4,701	4,728
30	30.40	30	4,242	4,268	4,292	4,317	4,341	4,366	4,390	4,416	4,441	4,466
29	28.80	29	4,005	4,029	4,052	4,076	4,100	4,122	4,146	4,170	4,194	4,218
28	27.27	28	3,780	3,801	3,824	3,846	3,869	3,890	3,913	3,936	3,960	3,982
27	25.80	27	3,565	3,586	3,608	3,628	3,649	3,672	3,693	3,714	3,736	3,758
26	24.40	26	3,361	3,381	3,401	3,421	3,441	3,461	3,482	3,502	3,523	3,544
25	23.07	25	3,168	3,186	3,205	3,224	3,244	3,263	3,283	3,301	3,321	3,341
24	21.80	24	2,984	3,001	3,020	3,038	3,056	3,074	3,093	3,112	3,130	3,149
23	20.60	23	2,809	2,826	2,842	2,860	2,877	2,894	2,913	2,930	2,948	2,965
22	19.45	22	2,644	2,660	2,676	2,692	2,709	2,725	2,742	2,758	2,776	2,792
21	18.35	21	2,486	2,502	2,517	2,533	2,548	2,564	2,580	2,596	2,612	2,628
20	17.31	20	2,338	2,352	2,366	2,381	2,395	2,410	2,426	2,441	2,456	2,472
19	16.33	19	2,197	2,210	2,224	2,238	2,252	2,266	2,280	2,294	2,309	2,324
18	15.40	18	2,064	2,076	2,089	2,102	2,116	2,129	2,142	2,156	2,169	2,182
17	14.50	17	1,937	1,949	1,961	1,974	1,986	2,000	2,013	2,025	2,037	2,050
16	13.65	16	1,817	1,829	1,841	1,853	1,865	1,877	1,889	1,901	1,913	1,925
15	12.85	15	1,705	1,716	1,727	1,739	1,749	1,760	1,772	1,783	1,796	1,806
14	12.09	14	1,598	1,608	1,619	1,629	1,640	1,651	1,661	1,672	1,683	1,694
13	11.37	13	1,497	1,507	1,517	1,527	1,537	1,547	1,557	1,567	1,577	1,588
12	10.68	12	1,403	1,412	1,421	1,431	1,440	1,449	1,459	1,468	1,477	1,487
11	10.03	11	1,312	1,321	1,330	1,339	1,348	1,357	1,366	1,375	1,384	1,393
10	9.41	10	1,228	1,236	1,244	1,252	1,261	1,269	1,277	1,286	1,295	1,304
9	8.83	9	1,148	1,156	1,164	1,172	1,179	1,187	1,195	1,203	1,212	1,220
8	8.28	8	1,072	1,080	1,087	1,095	1,102	1,109	1,117	1,125	1,132	1,140
7	7.76	7	1,001	1,008	1,016	1,023	1,030	1,037	1,044	1,051	1,058	1,065
6	7.27	6	935	941	948	955	961	968	975	981	988	995
5	6.80	5	872	879	885	891	897	903	909	916	922	928
4	6.37	4	813	819	825	831	836	842	848	854	860	866
3	5.96	3	757	762	768	774	780	785	791	796	802	808
2	5.57	2	705	710	716	721	727	732	737	742	747	752
1	5.20	1	657	661	666	671	676	681	685	690	695	700
0	4.85	0	611	615	620	624	628	633	637	642	647	652

WATER VAPOUR PRESSURE TABLE p_{sat} -20-0 °C

Water content of saturated air V_{sat} [g/m³]		Saturation pressure p_{sat} of the water vapour [Pa = N/m²] at a temperature of [°C]										
		$^1/_{10}$ °C	0.0	0.1	0.2	0.3	0.4	0.5	0.6	0.7	0.8	0.9
[°C]	[g/m³]	[°C]	[Pa]	[Pa]	[Pa]	[Pa]	[Pa]	[Pa]	[Pa]	[Pa]	[Pa]	[Pa]
0	4.85	-0	611	606	601	596	591	586	581	576	572	567
-1	4.49	-1	562	557	553	548	544	539	535	530	525	521
-2	4.14	-2	517	513	508	504	500	496	492	488	484	480
-3	3.82	-3	476	472	468	464	460	456	452	448	444	440
-4	3.52	-4	437	433	429	425	422	419	415	412	408	404
-5	3.25	-5	401	397	394	391	388	384	381	378	375	371
-6	2.99	-6	368	365	361	358	355	352	349	346	343	340
-7	2.75	-7	337	334	332	329	326	323	320	317	314	311
-8	2.53	-8	309	307	304	301	299	296	293	291	288	285
-9	2.33	-9	283	281	279	276	273	271	269	267	264	262
-10	2.14	-10	260	257	255	252	250	248	245	243	241	239
-11	1.97	-11	237	235	233	231	229	227	225	223	221	219
-12	1.81	-12	217	215	213	211	209	207	205	203	201	199
-13	1.66	-13	198	196	195	193	191	189	187	185	184	182
-14	1.52	-14	181	179	177	176	175	173	171	169	168	166
-15	1.39	-15	165	164	163	161	159	157	156	154	153	152
-16	1.27	-16	151	149	148	147	145	144	142	141	140	139
-17	1.16	-17	137	136	135	133	132	131	130	129	127	125
-18	1.06	-18	124	123	122	121	120	119	117	116	115	114
-19	0.97	-19	113	112	111	110	109	108	107	105	104	103
-20	0.88	-20	102	101	100	99	99	98	97	96	95	94

SURFACE CONDENSATION

Internal surface temperature θ_{si} equal to or lower than the dew point temperature θ_D of the ambient air:

$\theta_{si} \leq \theta_D$

where

$p = p_{sat}(\theta_{si}) \rightarrow \varphi = 100\%$

MOULD GROWTH – CAPILLARY CONDENSATION

can already happen if the surface temperature θ_{si} corresponds to the dew point of the air at 80% relative humidity:

$p = 0.8 \cdot p_{sat}(\theta_{si})$

Temperature dependence

For surface condensation and mould growth, the lowest actual surface temperature θ_{si} in a room is relevant

TEMPERATURE FACTOR f_{Rsi} [–]

for computing the internal surface temperature θ_{si} at a given temperature difference between room air and external temperature

$f_{Rsi} = \dfrac{\theta_{si} - \theta_e}{\theta_i - \theta_e} \cong 1 - R_i \cdot U$ [–] [dimensionless]

θ_e: External temperature
θ_i: Internal or room temperature
θ_{si}: Internal surface temperature
R_i: Internal heat transfer resistance
U: Heat transfer coefficient

To check the risk of mould growth and surface condensation, more severe conditions are applied: → use safety values for R_i

Safety values $R_{i,sv}$

Increase of heat transfer resistance:
$R_i \rightarrow R_{i,sv}$
Decrease of internal heat transfer coefficient:
$h_i \rightarrow h_{i,sv}$

For windows, doors:
$R_{i,sv} = 0.15$ [m²K/W]; $h_{i,sv} = 6.67$ [W/m²K]

Upper part of the room:
$R_{i,sv} = 0.25$ [m²K/W]; $h_{i,sv} = 4.0$ [W/m²K]

Lower part of the room:
$R_{i,sv} = 0.35$ [m²K/W]; $h_{i,sv} = 2.86$ [W/m²K]

Comparison:
Standard for U-value computation
$R_{i,sv} = 0.125$ [m²K/W]; $h_{i,sv} = 8.0$ [W/m²K])

COMPUTATION OF MINIMUM ADMISSIBLE f_{Rsi}

Necessary if the exisiting temperature factor f_{Rsi} of thermal bridges < 0.75 or if the humidity is higher than normal.

1. External climate

Determination of air temperature and humidity
Surface condensation $\theta_{e,min}$, $p_{e,min}$
Mould growth $\theta_{e,min}$, $p_{e,min}$

2. Internal climate

Determination of room temperature θ_i and humidity p_i
Safety surcharge for the vapour pressure:
$p^+_{i,max} = 1.25\ p_{i,max} - 0.25\ p_e$

3. Determination

of acceptable minimum surface temperature
$\theta_{si,min} \rightarrow \theta_{si,min} = \theta_D$, dew point temperature

Surface condensation at θ_D to $p^+_{i,max}$
Free of mould at θ_D to $1.25 \cdot p^+_{i,max}$
or $p^+_{i,max}/0.8$

4. Computation

of minimum admissible temperature factor $f_{Rsi,min}$

$f_{Rsi,min} = \dfrac{\theta_{si,min} - \theta_e}{\theta_i - \theta_e}$

5. Check

whether the following condition is satisfied:
$f_{Rsi} > f_{Rsi,min}$

PROTECTION AGAINST MOISTURE

If the following conditions for the U_{max}-value [W/m²K] of building elements without thermal bridges are fulfilled, a computed check of surface condensation/mould growth need not be done:

Building element	U_{max} [W/m²K], building element against		
	External climate/ up to 2 m in the earth	Unheated rooms	More than 2 m in the earth
Roof, pitched/flat	0.4	0.5	0.6
Wall	0.4	0.6	0.6
Windows, doors	2.4	2.4	–
Floor	0.4	0.6	0.6

Thermal bridges require no proof if their temperature factor $f_{R_{si}} \geq 0.75$

AVOIDING MOULD GROWTH/SURFACE CONDENSATION
Check-up scheme

Water vapour curves

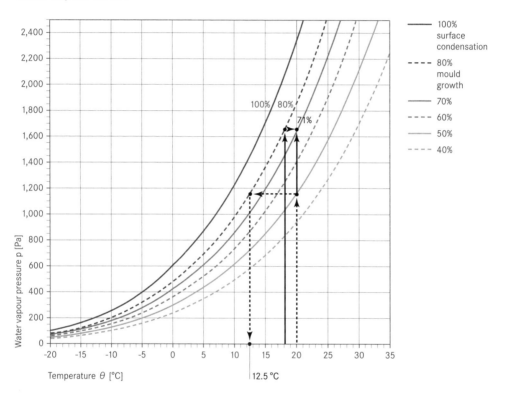

known: θ_i, θ_e, φ ┈┈┈┈┈┈➤ θ_{si} ┈┈┈┈┈┈➤ $f_{Rsi} = \dfrac{\theta_{si} - \theta_e}{\theta_i - \theta_e}$ ┈┈┈

sought: φ ◀┈┈┈┈┈ θ_{si} ◀┈┈┈┈┈ $\theta_{si} = \theta_e + f_{Rsi} \cdot (\theta_i - \theta_e)$ ◀┈┈

Example:

$\theta_i = 20\ °C$, $\theta_e = -4\ °C$, $\varphi = 50\%$ ┈┈┈┈➤ $\theta_{si} = 12.5\ °C$ ┈┈┈➤ $f_{Rsi} = \dfrac{12.5 - (-4)}{20 - (-4)} = \dfrac{16.5}{24} = 0.6875$ ┈┈┈┈

$\varphi = 71\%$ ◀┈┈┈┈┈ $\theta_{si} = 18.04\ °C$ ◀┈ $\theta_{si} = -8 + 0.93 \cdot (20 - (-8)) = 18.04\ °C$ ◀┈

Temperature factor curve (exact)

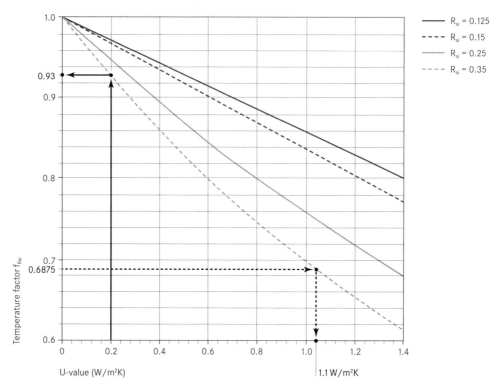

R$_{si}$ = 0.125
R$_{si}$ = 0.15
R$_{si}$ = 0.25
R$_{si}$ = 0.35

Temperature factor f$_{Rsi}$

U-value (W/m²K)

1.1 W/m²K

f$_{Rsi}$ ··► sought: U

f$_{Rsi}$ ◄──────────── known: U, θ_e, θ_i

f$_{Rsi}$ = 0.6875 ································► U-value = 1.1 W/m²K

f$_{Rsi}$ = 0.93 ◄──────────── U = 0.2 W/m²K, θ_i = 20 °C, θ_e = -8 °C

WATER VAPOUR DIFFUSION

Through porous building components and layer structures, water vapour diffusion has to be controlled to avoid condensation within a construction.

A WATER VAPOUR CONDUCTIVITY δ
$[mg/h \cdot m \cdot Pa]$
depending on material

Air at 20 °C:
$$\delta_a = 0.72 \left[\frac{mg}{h \cdot m \cdot Pa} \right]$$

DIFFUSION RESISTANCE FIGURE μ [–]
$$\mu = \frac{\delta_a}{\delta}$$
depending on material
see annex

B DIFFUSION EQUIVALENT AIR LAYER s [m]
$s = \mu \cdot d$ [m]

Air layer s with the same diffusion resistance as the corresponding material layer

A WATER VAPOUR CONDUCTIVITY δ_a OF STILL AIR

Values for water vapour conducitvity δ_a [mg/h · m · Pa] of air at		
θ (°C)	p = 1,013 mbar	p = 945 mbar
+30	0.695	0.745
+20	0.677	0.720
+10	0.658	0.705
0	0.639	0.685
-10	0.620	0.655
-20	0.600	0.644

B DIFFUSION EQUIVALENT AIR LAYER s OF SOME MATERIALS

	d	μ	s
Aluminium foil	> 25 μm	–	vapour-proof, ∞
PVC foil	> 0.1 mm	20,000	> 2 m
Concrete	0.2 m	100	20 m
Bonded wooden panel	0.04 m	140	5.6 m
Natural wood	0.07 m	20	1.4 m
Ceramic tile	0.005 m	300	1.5 m
Brick	0.15 m	4	0.6 m
Plasterboard	0.0125 m	5	0.06 m
Interior plaster	0.02 m	6	0.12 m

C CONDENSATION CHECK-UP
after Glaser, graphic tool
Comparison of temperature profile and vapour pressure profile in a construction to see whether the temperature profile will interfere with the vapour pressure profile.

After Helmut Glaser
SIA 180/EN ISO 13788

Exterior:
Temperature θ_e
Vapour pressure p_e

Interior:
Temperature θ_i
Vapour pressure p_i
according to user conditions

INSULATING MATERIALS WITH HIGH DIFFUSION RESISTANCE

Example 1
Construction using:
External plaster 0.02 m
Polystyrene 0.15 m
Brick 0.15 m
Internal plaster 0.01 m

Exterior:
Temperature θ_e = -10 °C
Relative humidity φ = 80%

Interior:
Temperature θ_i = +20 °C
Relative humidity φ = 70%

C CONDENSATION CHECK-UP
after Glaser, graphic tool

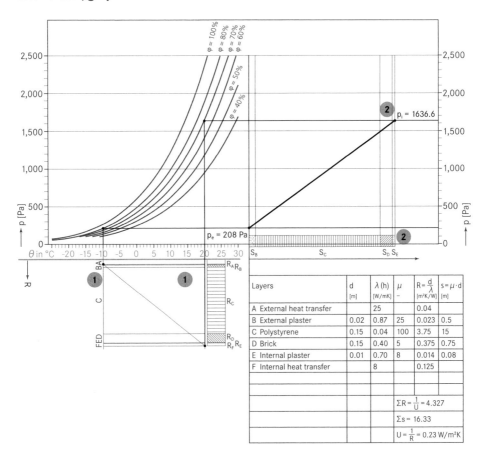

Layers	d [m]	λ (h) [W/mK]	μ –	$R = \frac{d}{\lambda}$ [m²K/W]	$s = \mu \cdot d$ [m]
A External heat transfer		25		0.04	
B External plaster	0.02	0.87	25	0.023	0.5
C Polystyrene	0.15	0.04	100	3.75	15
D Brick	0.15	0.40	5	0.375	0.75
E Internal plaster	0.01	0.70	8	0.014	0.08
F Internal heat transfer		8		0.125	
				$\Sigma R = \frac{1}{U} = 4.327$	
				$\Sigma s = 16.33$	
				$U = \frac{1}{R} = 0.23$ W/m²K	

1   Enter layer structure in the scale of thermal resistances
    Straight line between internal and external temperatures yields temperatures at layer
    boundaries.
2   Enter layer structure in the scale of the diffusion equivalent air layers
    Straight line between internal and external vapour pressure yields undisturbed vapour
    pressures at layer boundaries.

CONDENSATION CHECK-UP
after Glaser, graphic tool

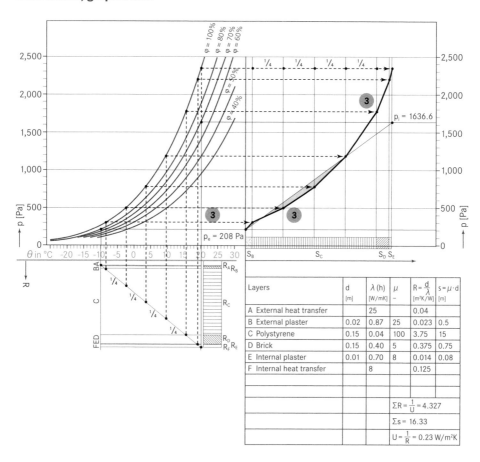

Layers	d	λ (h)	μ	R = d/λ	s = μ·d
	[m]	[W/mK]	–	[m²K/W]	[m]
A External heat transfer		25		0.04	
B External plaster	0.02	0.87	25	0.023	0.5
C Polystyrene	0.15	0.04	100	3.75	15
D Brick	0.15	0.40	5	0.375	0.75
E Internal plaster	0.01	0.70	8	0.014	0.08
F Internal heat transfer		8		0.125	
				$\Sigma R = \frac{1}{U} = 4.327$	
				$\Sigma s = 16.33$	
				$U = \frac{1}{R} = 0.23$ W/m²K	

3 Transfer the layer boundary temperatures via the 100% humidity curve to lines of the diffusion equivalent air layers s. The intersections show the saturation pressure profile at the layer boundaries.
Insulation materials with large diffusion resistances show a "curved" vapour profile.
It can be approximated by constructing intermediate points at ¼, ⅛ etc. of the important layer. The resulting polygon is a good approximation of the real vapour curve.

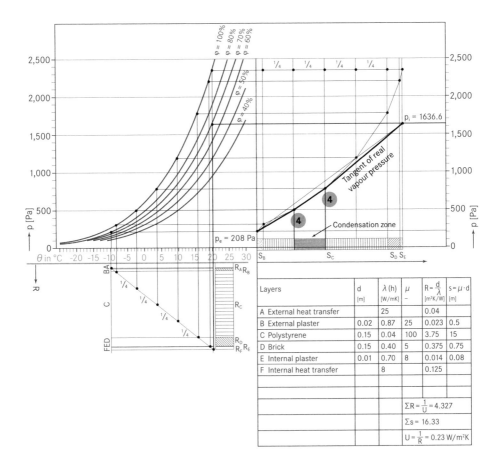

Layers	d [m]	λ (h) [W/mK]	μ –	R = $\frac{d}{\lambda}$ [m²K/W]	s = μ·d [m]
A External heat transfer		25		0.04	
B External plaster	0.02	0.87	25	0.023	0.5
C Polystyrene	0.15	0.04	100	3.75	15
D Brick	0.15	0.40	5	0.375	0.75
E Internal plaster	0.01	0.70	8	0.014	0.08
F Internal heat transfer		8		0.125	
				$\sum R = \frac{1}{U} = 4.327$	
				$\sum s = 16.33$	
				$U = \frac{1}{R} = 0.23$ W/m²K	

4 No intersection between saturation pressure profile and undisturbed pressure profile:
→ no condensation to be expected

If there is an intersection → condensation must be expected:
Set the tangents from the the internal and external starting points onto the saturation profile
to obtain the actual vapour pressure profile → extension of condensation zone

INSULATING MATERIALS WITH LOW DIFFUSION RESISTANCE

Example 2
Construction using
External plaster 0.02 m
Brick 0.12 m
Rockwool (90 kg/m^3) 0.10 m
Brick 0.175 m
Internal plaster 0.01 m

Exterior:
Temperature θ_e = -10 °C
Relative humidity φ = 80%

Interior:
Temperature θ_i = +20 °C
Relative humidity φ = 50%

SIA 180/EN ISO 13788

CONDENSATION CHECK-UP
after Glaser, graphic tool

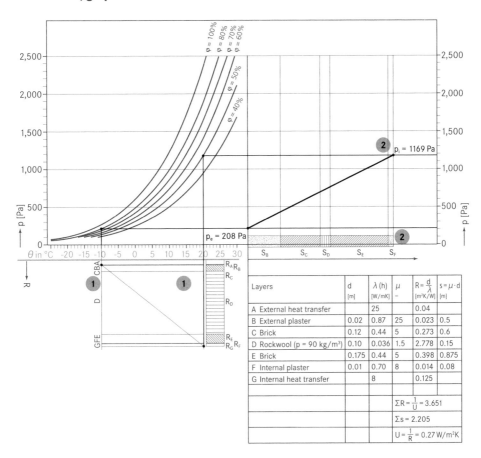

Layers	d [m]	λ (h) [W/mK]	μ –	$R = \frac{d}{\lambda}$ [m²K/W]	$s = \mu \cdot d$ [m]
A External heat transfer		25		0.04	
B External plaster	0.02	0.87	25	0.023	0.5
C Brick	0.12	0.44	5	0.273	0.6
D Rockwool (p = 90 kg/m³)	0.10	0.036	1.5	2.778	0.15
E Brick	0.175	0.44	5	0.398	0.875
F Internal plaster	0.01	0.70	8	0.014	0.08
G Internal heat transfer		8		0.125	
				$\Sigma R = \frac{1}{U} = 3.651$	
				$\Sigma s = 2.205$	
				$U = \frac{1}{R} = 0.27\,W/m^2K$	

1 Enter layer structure in the scale of heat resistances.
A straight line between internal and external temperature yields temperatures at all layer boundaries.
2 The straight line between internal and external vapour pressure yields vapour pressures at all layer boundaries → undisturbed vapour pressure profile

CONDENSATION CHECK-UP
after Glaser, graphic tool

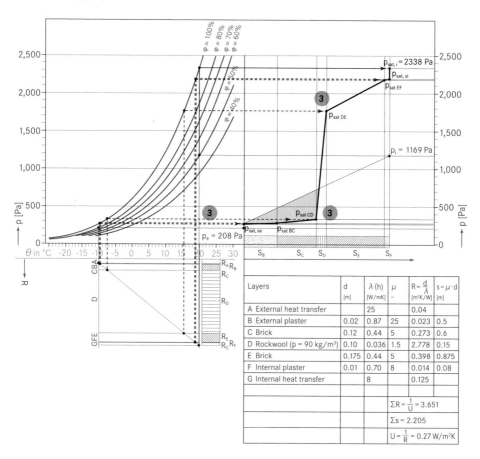

Layers	d [m]	λ (h) [W/mK]	μ –	R = $\frac{d}{\lambda}$ [m²K/W]	s = μ·d [m]
A External heat transfer		25		0.04	
B External plaster	0.02	0.87	25	0.023	0.5
C Brick	0.12	0.44	5	0.273	0.6
D Rockwool (p = 90 kg/m³)	0.10	0.036	1.5	2.778	0.15
E Brick	0.175	0.44	5	0.398	0.875
F Internal plaster	0.01	0.70	8	0.014	0.08
G Internal heat transfer		8		0.125	
				$\Sigma R = \frac{1}{U} = 3.651$	
				$\Sigma s = 2.205$	
				$U = \frac{1}{R} = 0.27\ W/m^2K$	

3 Transfer the layer boundary temperatures via the 100% humidity curve to lines of the diffusion equivalent air layers s. The intersections show the saturation pressure profile at the layer boundaries.

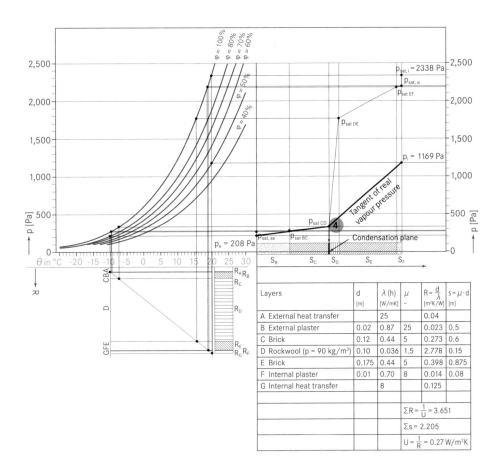

Layers	d [m]	λ (h) [W/mK]	μ –	$R = \dfrac{d}{\lambda}$ [m²K/W]	$s = \mu \cdot d$ [m]
A External heat transfer		25		0.04	
B External plaster	0.02	0.87	25	0.023	0.5
C Brick	0.12	0.44	5	0.273	0.6
D Rockwool (p = 90 kg/m³)	0.10	0.036	1.5	2.778	0.15
E Brick	0.175	0.44	5	0.398	0.875
F Internal plaster	0.01	0.70	8	0.014	0.08
G Internal heat transfer		8		0.125	
				$\Sigma R = \dfrac{1}{U} = 3.651$	
				$\Sigma s = 2.205$	
				$U = \dfrac{1}{R} = 0.27\ \text{W/m}^2\text{K}$	

4   No intersection between the saturation pressure profile and the undisturbed pressure profile:
→ no condensation to be expected

If there is an intersection → condensation must be expected:
Set the tangents from the internal and external starting points onto the saturation profile to obtain the actual vapour pressure profile; "break-point" on the profile → condensation plane instead of a zone in this case

AMOUNT OF CONDENSATE CHECK-UP
after Glaser, numeric computation
Assumption of a so-called "block climate"
for condensation and drying period
with the following constant conditions
for winter and summer:

Winter:
Duration of condensation period 1,440 h = 60 d
depending on climate
Internal: θ_i = +20 °C, φ = 50%
External: θ_e = -10 °C, φ = 80%

Amount of condensate g_c [g/m²]

$$g_c = \delta_a \left[\frac{p_i - p_{sat}}{s_i} - \frac{p_{sat} - p_e}{s_e} \right] \cdot \frac{1440}{1000} \ [g/m^2]$$

where:
diffusion equivalent air layer s_i from the
internal surface to the condensation layer

Summer:
Duration of drying period 2,160 h = 90 d
depending on climate
Internal: θ_i = 12 °C, φ = 70%
External: θ_e = 12 °C, φ = 70%

Drying potential g_{ev} [g/m²]

$$g_{ev} = \delta_a \left[\frac{p_{sat} - p_i}{s_i} + \frac{p_{sat} - p_e}{s_e} \right] \cdot \frac{2160}{1000} \ [g/m^2]$$

where:
diffusion equivalent air layer s_e from the
condensation layer to the external surface

if:
drying potential $g_{ev} \geq$ amount of condensate g_c
→ the building element has dried out again
after a one-year cycle.

EXAMPLE
Condensation plane – see example graphic tool pages 124–127

Layer		d [m]	μ [–]	$s = \mu \cdot d$ [m]
B	External plaster	0.02	25	0.5
C	Brick	0.12	5	0.6
D	Rockwool (90 kg/m³)	0.10	1.5	0.15
E	Brick	0.175	5	0.875
F	Internal plaster	0.01	8	0.08

$s_e = 1.1$ m

Condensation plane -7.0 °C

$s_i = 1.105$ m

Amount of condensate g_c
from the inner surface to the condensation plane
duration of condensation period in winter, 1,440 h = 60 d
internal: $\theta_i = +20$ °C, $\varphi = 50\%$
external: $\theta_e = -10$ °C, $\varphi = 80\%$
δ_a: see table page 119

From vapour pressure table:
$p_i = 2{,}338$ Pa $\cdot 0.5$
$p_e = 260 \cdot 0.8$ Pa
$p_{sat} = 337$ Pa at condensation plane -7.0 °C

$$g_c = \delta_a \left[\frac{p_i - p_{sat}}{s_i} - \frac{p_{sat} - p_e}{s_e} \right] \cdot \frac{1440}{1000} \ [g/m^2]$$

$$= 0.72 \left[\frac{2338 \cdot 0.5 - 337}{1.105} - \frac{337 - 260 \cdot 0.8}{1.1} \right] \cdot \frac{1440}{1000}$$

$$= 659.1 \ [g/m^2]$$

Drying potential g_{ev}
from the condensation plane to the external surface
duration of drying period in summer, 2,160 h = 90 d
internal: $\theta_i = 12$ °C, $\varphi = 70\%$
external: $\theta_e = 12$ °C, $\varphi = 70\%$

$$g_{ev} = \delta_a \left[\frac{p_{sat} - p_i}{s_i} + \frac{p_{sat} - p_e}{s_e} \right] \cdot \frac{2160}{1000} \ [g/m^2]$$

$$= 0.66 \left[\frac{1403 - 1403 \cdot 0.7}{1.105} + \frac{1403 - 1403 \cdot 0.7}{1.1} \right] \cdot \frac{2160}{1000}$$

$$= 1{,}088.5 \ [g/m^2]$$

Drying potential g_{ev} > amount of condensate g_c
→ the building element has dried out again after a one-year cycle.

DESIGN PRINCIPLES FOR CONSTRUCTION

BASIC ORDER OF CONSTRUCTION LAYERS

High diffusion resistances
always on the warm side of the layer structure
→ reduces vapour pressure as soon as possible

High thermal resistances
always on the cold side of the layer structure
→ keeps temperature high as long as possible

Basic aim:
Choice of construction/layer structure without risk of mould growth or condensation

Amount of condensate/drying period
If it is impossible to construction without risk of condensation, Glaser's method can be used to check whether the condensate that has arisen can dry out again in the dry period.
If this condition is fulfilled: → ok

Simulation software (e.g. WUFI, DELPHIN) is recommended in critical cases.

A Limitation of damage
Definition of a limited amount of condensation that may occur during the condensation period.

A Limitation of damage
Acceptable maximum amount of condensate

Material	Amount of condensate
Insulating materials	< 1 % layer volume
Wood	< 3 % layer mass
Timber materials	< 3 % layer mass
Porous materials with capillary transport	< 0.8 kg/m^2

SIA 180, 6.3.2.4

SOUND DIMENSION

A AUDIBLE FREQUENCY RANGE
From 20 Hz to 20 kHz

AUDIBLE WAVELENGTH RANGE IN AIR
Wavelength L from 1.7 cm to 17 m

INTENSITY RANGE
Intensity I from 10^{-12} W/m² to 1 W/m²

ULTRASOUND
Frequencies above the audible range

INFRASOUND
Frequencies below the audible range

SOUND VELOCITY
Air 0 °C: 332 m/s
Air 15 °C: 341 m/s
Water: 1,480 m/s
Concrete: 3,500–4,000 m/s
Steel: 4,800–5,000 m/s
Wood: 3,500–5,000 m/s
Glass: 5,100–5,500 m/s

B SOUND LEVEL L [dB]
of a sound wave with a sound pressure amplitude p_o

$$L = 10 \log \left(\frac{I}{I_{ref}}\right) = 20 \log \left(\frac{p_o}{p_{ref}}\right) \text{[dB]}$$

when:

$$I_{ref} = 10^{-12} \frac{W}{m^2} \quad \text{or} \quad p_{ref} = 2 \cdot 10^{-5} \text{ Pa}$$

Increase of sound level L
by 3 dB if intensity is doubled

by 6 dB if sound pressure is doubled

A AUDIBLE FREQUENCY RANGE

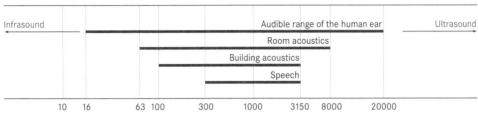

Frequency f [Hz]

B SOUND LEVEL L, SOUND PRESSURE p AND SOUND INTENSITY I
for different noises

Source	Distance [m]	Sensation	Sound level L [dB]	Sound pressure p [Pa]	Sound intensity I [W/m²]
Propeller-driven aeroplane	5	unbearable	130	63	10
Air hammer	1	unbearable	120	20	1
Boiler shop	–	unbearable	110	6.3	$100 \cdot 10^{-3}$
Car horn, klaxon	5	very loud	100	2	$10 \cdot 10^{-3}$
Lorry	5	very loud	90	$630 \cdot 10^{-3}$	$1 \cdot 10^{-3}$
Loud radio music	–	very loud	80	$200 \cdot 10^{-3}$	$100 \cdot 10^{-6}$
Conversation	1	loud	70	$63 \cdot 10^{-3}$	$10 \cdot 10^{-6}$
Car	10	loud	60	$20 \cdot 10^{-3}$	$1 \cdot 10^{-6}$
Quiet stream or river	–	low	50	$6 \cdot 10^{-3}$	$100 \cdot 10^{-9}$
Residential area without traffic	–	low	40	$2 \cdot 10^{-3}$	$10 \cdot 10^{-9}$
Quiet garden	–	very low	30	$630 \cdot 10^{-6}$	$1 \cdot 10^{-9}$
Pocket watch	–	very low	20	$200 \cdot 10^{-6}$	$100 \cdot 10^{-12}$
Imperceptible	–	inaudible	10	$63 \cdot 10^{-6}$	$10 \cdot 10^{-12}$
Absolute silence	–	inaudible	0	$20 \cdot 10^{-6}$	$1 \cdot 10^{-12}$

SPREAD OF SOUND

SOUND EMISSION LEVEL
TRAFFIC

A Cars

Equivalent permanent noise level of car traffic at 25 m from the middle of the street, according to traffic density

B Lorries

Equivalent permanent noise level of lorry traffic at 25 m from the middle of the street, according to traffic density

In both cases, the parameter speed is given in km/h.

A Cars

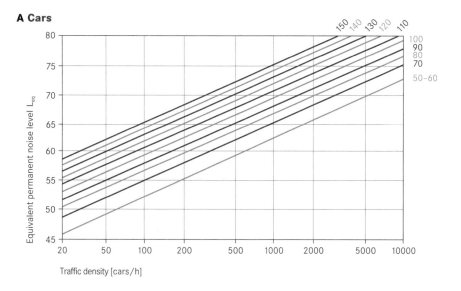

B Lorries

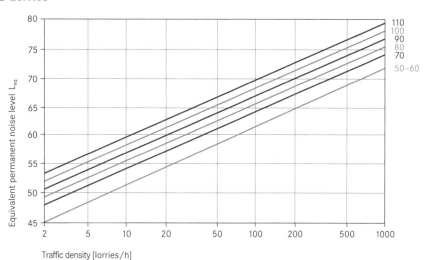

NOISE PROTECTION REGULATION
LIMITATIONS FOR EXTERNAL NOISE IMPACT
Noise Abatement Ordinance (NAO) 814.41; version 2006
see EU Directive 2002/49/EC, 25.6.2002

	Planning level L_r [dB(A)]		Immission level limit L_r [dB(A)]		Alarm value L_r [dB(A)]	
Sensitivity levels	Day	Night	Day	Night	Day	Night
I Recreational zone	50	40	55	45	65	60
II Residential zone	55	45	60	50	70	65
III Residential and trade zone	60	50	65	55	70	65
IV Industrial zone	65	55	70	60	75	70

REQUIREMENTS

	Planning level	Immission level limit	Alarm value
New noise emitting industries	→ Compliance		
Relevant changes to existing industry	→	→ No exceeding	
→ Existing industry must be remediated	←	If exceeded	
→ Noise protection measures necessary, to be compensated	←	←	May only be exceeded for public needs or by licensed industries

DISTANCE DEPENDENCY
Noise level L(r) as function of distance r from source

	Point source	Linear source
Free space	$L(r) = L_0 - 20 \cdot \log(r) - 11$ dB	
Half space, on a plane	$L(r) = L_0 - 20 \cdot \log(r) - 8$ dB	$L(r) = L_0 - 10 \cdot \log(r) - 5$ dB
Quarter space, in front of a house, embankment	$L(r) = L_0 - 20 \cdot \log(r) - 5$ dB	$L(r) = L_0 - 10 \cdot \log(r) - 2$ dB
Eighth space, in a corner	$L(r) = L_0 - 20 \cdot \log(r) - 2$ dB	
Doubling of distance	-6 dB $= 20 \cdot \log(2)$	-3 dB $= 10 \cdot \log(2)$

C (marginal label)

L_0 = Source level at 1 m from source = sound power level

Note

$\log(u \cdot v) = \log u + \log v$

$\log\left(\dfrac{u}{v}\right) = \log u - \log v$

$\log\left(\dfrac{1}{v}\right) = -\log v$

$\log(u^r) = r \cdot \log u$

$x = 10^{\log x}$

Note

A heavily frequented road has to be considered as a linear source. The noise decreases less quickly with increasing distance from the noise source, see doubling of distance.

C Decrease of sound level ΔL in half space

known:
Noise source
Data at first measuring point
Distance of new measuring point from noise source

Point source: $\Delta L = L_1 - L_2 = 20 \cdot \log \dfrac{r_2}{r_1}$

Linear source: $\Delta L = 10 \cdot \log \dfrac{r_2}{r_1}$

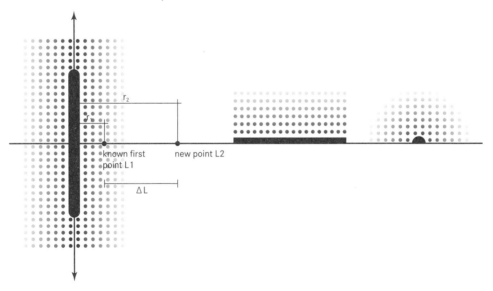

Floor plan   Longitudinal section   Cross section

D EFFECT OF OBSTACLES
DECREASE OF NOISE LEVEL ΔL [dB]

Behind a building: D_z

$\Delta L = D_z = 10 \cdot \log (3 + 6 \cdot 10^{-2} \cdot f \cdot z)$ [dB]

D_z = Decrease of the level [dB]

f = Frequency [Hz]

z = Shielding distance value [m]

with

$$z \cong \frac{h_{eff}^2}{2} \cdot \left(\frac{1}{S_Q} + \frac{1}{S_I} \right) \text{ [m]}$$

Behind a building

ΔL = -15 to -25 dB

On the side of a building

ΔL = -5 to -10 dB

Absorption by air

ΔL = -0.5 dB for every 100 m

Vegetation

ΔL = -0.05 dB for every 1 m for the range 20–200 m

Noise protection wall, embankment

see graphs on pages 144–151

D EFFECT OF OBSTACLES
DECREASE OF NOISE LEVEL ΔL [dB]
behind a building

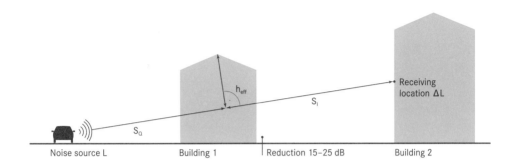

Noise source L   Building 1   Reduction 15–25 dB   Building 2

h_{eff}

S_Q

S_I

Receiving
location ΔL

E NOISE PROTECTION EMBANKMENT
Reduction of traffic noise on a double-lane road

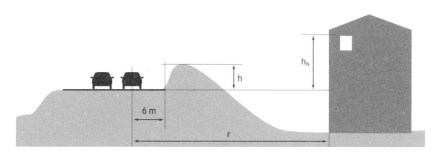

Reduction of the equivalent permanent noise level through a noise protection embankment by a double-lane road.
Parameter: Height of embankment h [m]

E NOISE PROTECTION EMBANKMENT
Reduction of traffic noise on a double-lane road

r = 25 m

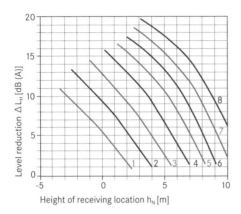

r = 50 m

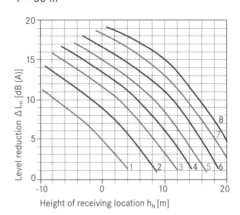

r = 100 m

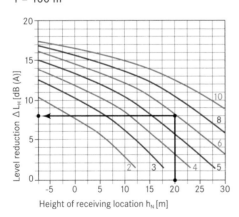

r = 200 m

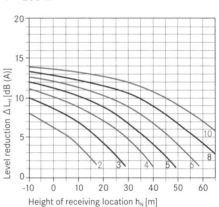

F NOISE PROTECTION EMBANKMENT
Reduction of traffic noise on a four-lane road

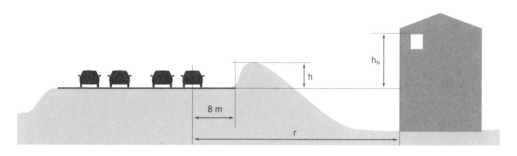

Reduction of the equivalent permanent noise level through a noise protection embankment by a four-lane road.
Parameter: Height of embankment h [m]

F NOISE PROTECTION EMBANKMENT
Reduction of traffic noise on a four-lane road

r = 25 m

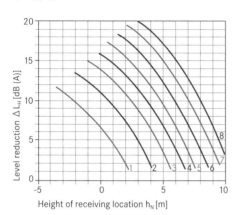

r = 50 m

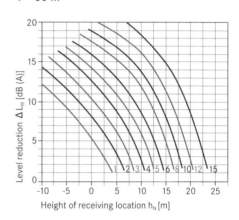

r = 100 m

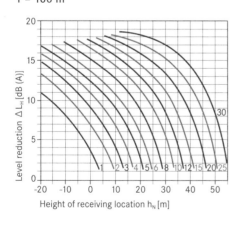

r = 200 m

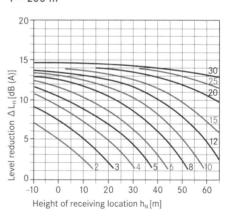

G NOISE PROTECTION WALL
Reduction of traffic noise on a double-lane road

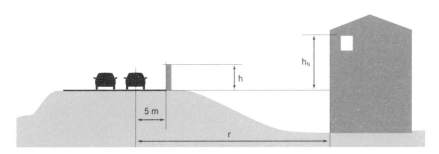

Reduction of the equivalent noise level through a noise protection wall by a double-lane road.
Parameter: Wall height h [m]

G NOISE PROTECTION WALL
Reduction of traffic noise on a double-lane road

r = 25 m

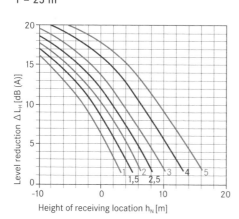

r = 50 m

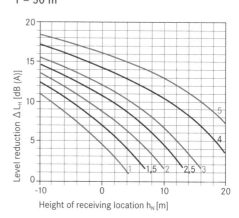

r = 100 m

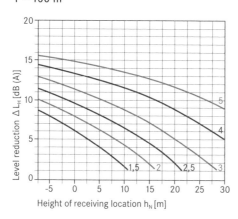

r = 200 m

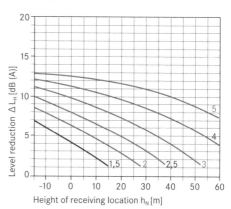

H NOISE PROTECTION WALL
Reduction of traffic noise on a four-lane road

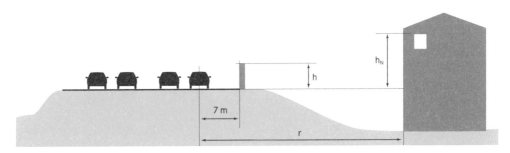

Reduction of the equivalent permanent noise level through a noise protection wall by a four-lane road. Parameter: Wall height h [m]

H NOISE PROTECTION WALL
Reduction of traffic noise on a four-lane road

r = 25 m

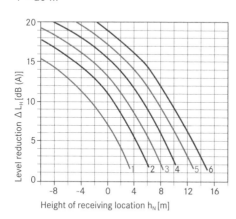

r = 50 m

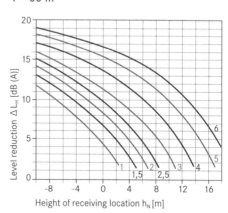

r = 100 m

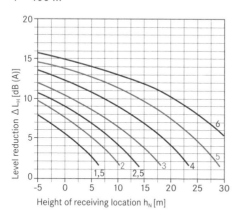

r = 200 m

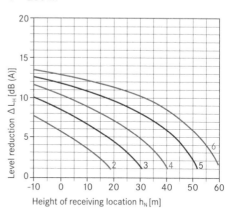

LOWERING OF STREET LEVEL
Reduction of traffic noise depending on depth

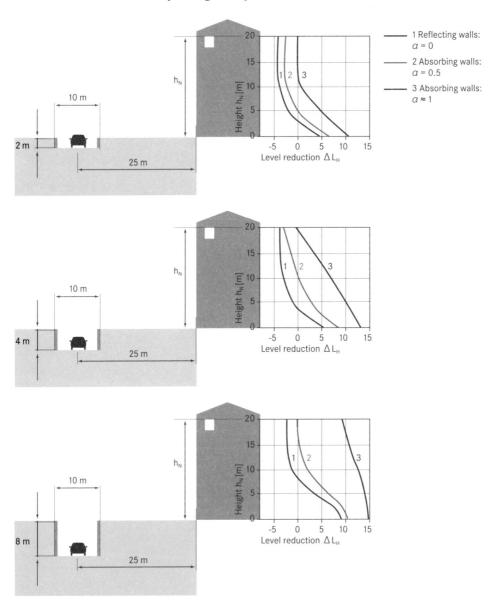

AIRBORNE AND IMPACT SOUND

Airborne sound
The protection from airborne sound is the better, the greater the standard noise level difference is. Values describe building components as "noise filters".

Impact sound
The protection from impact sound is the better, the lower the maximum acceptable standard impact sound level is. Values describe the "noise pollution" in the receiving rooms.

DETERMINATION OF NOISE PROTECTION against airborne noise
SIA 181

A 1. Determine noise sensitivity level of receiver
L_{RL} = required level: low – medium – high

B 2. Determine noise source intensity qualitatively
or from noise cadastre
L_{NL} = noise level = L_r

C 3. Standard noise level difference → required values $D_{e,i}$
$D_{e,i} = L_{NL} - L_{RL}$

4. Compute volume V of receiving room and size of the common surface S

D 5. Determine necessary noise level correction ΔL_{AS} from nomogram
or
$$\Delta L_{AS} = 10 \log \left(\frac{V}{S}\right) - 4.9 \text{ dB}$$

E Volume related correction C_V from table

6. Corrected required noise protection measure R'$_w$
$R'_w + C \geq D_{e,i} - \Delta L_{AS} + C_V$
$R'_w + C$: specific, depends on building component

7. Spectral adaptation C and C_{tr} of internal and external noise
C: Spectral correction for internal noise
$R'_w + C \geq D_i - \Delta L_{AS} + C_V$
C_{tr}: Spectral correction for external noise
$R'_w + C_{tr} \geq D_e - \Delta L_{AS} + C_V$

Example: Bedroom next to living room

1. Bedroom = receiving room
L_{RL} = medium

2. Living room = emitting room
L_{NL} = medium
Minimum requirements to counter internal noise

3. Requirement for partition wall
D_i = 52 dB

4. Receiving room bedroom
V = 25.2 m³ (e.g.)
Common surface of partition wall
S = 8.4 m² (e.g.)

5. Nomogram for necessary noise level correction ΔL_{AS}
or
$$\Delta L_{AS} = 10 \log \left(\frac{25.2}{8.4}\right) - 4.9 \text{ dB} = -0.13 \text{ dB}$$
with volume related correction C_V = 0

6. Corrected required noise protection measure R'$_w$
$R'_w + C \geq 52 - (-0.13) + 0 = 52.13$ dB

7. Possible wall construction:
Calmo brick wall, with internal plaster thickness d = 20 cm
$R'_w + C = 55 + (-2) = 53$ dB

R'_w and C:
see manufacturers' data
see annex

SENSITIVITY TO AIRBORNE AND IMPACT SOUND

	Sensitivity L_{RL}	Use of receiving room
A	low < 35 dB	Dense occupation, mainly manual work or only short-term use: workshop, open-plan office, kitchen, canteen, laboratory, corridor etc.
	medium < 30 dB	Intellectual work, living, sleeping: living or bedroom, apartment, classroom, music room, office, hotel, hospital ward etc.
	high < 25 dB	Special need for quiet: rest area in hospital, special treatment room, music studio etc.

SIA 181, 2.3

MINIMUM REQUIREMENTS FOR INTERNAL AIRBORNE SOUND

	Noise source intensity	low	medium	high *	very high **
B	Emitting room	Low-level use	Normal use	Noisy use	Very noisy use
	Examples	Reading room, waiting room, ward, archive etc.	Living room, bedroom, bath, toilet, kitchen, corridor, elevator, staircase, meeting room, laboratory, sales room etc.	Rec room, meeting room, classroom, kindergarten, restaurant without music, salesroom with music, heating room, garage, machine room etc.	Trade, workshop, factory, music practice room, gym, restaurant with music etc.
C	Noise sensitivity	Required values for standard noise level difference D_i**			
	low	42 dB	47 dB	52 dB	57 dB
	medium	47 dB	52 dB	57 dB	62 dB
	high	52 dB	57 dB	62 dB	67 dB

* Special uses (SIA 181, subparagraph 3.2.1.4)
** Special regulations for entrances (SIA 181, subparagraph 3.2.1.5)

Where requirements for protection from airborne sound are increased, the values of the standard level difference "minimum requirements" are increased by 3 dB, to counter internal and external sources.

SIA 181, 3.2.1.2

MINIMUM REQUIREMENTS TO PROTECT FROM EXTERNAL AIRBORNE SOUND

B **Noise source intensity**	**Degree of external disturbance**			
	Low to moderate		**Considerable to very strong**	
Location of receiving room	Away from traffic, no noisy industry		Near to traffic or noisy industry	
Period of sensitivity	Day	Night	Day	Night
Noise level dB(A)	$L_r \leq 60$	$L_r \leq 52$	$L_r > 60$	$L_r > 52$
C **Noise sensitivity**	**Requirements for standard noise level difference D_e**			
low	22 dB	22 dB	$L_r - 38$ dB	$L_r - 30$ dB
medium	27 dB	27 dB	$L_r - 33$ dB	$L_r - 25$ dB
high	32 dB	32 dB	$L_r - 28$ dB	$L_r - 20$ dB

SIA 181, 3.1.1.2

EXAMPLES OF THE MINIMUM REQUIREMENTS TO PROTECT FROM INTERNAL AIRBORNE SOUND D_{i50} FOR ROOMS WITH MUSIC

Noise level impact	Moderate	Considerable	Strong	Very strong
Examples of emitting venues	Restaurant, coffee shop with increased noise level	Pub, bar	Nightclub, or similar venue with very high noise level	Disco, dancing, live music
$L_{Aeq(t)}$ dB (A)	from 75–80	from 80–85	from 85–90	> 90
Noise sensitivity	**Range of requirements for the standard noise level difference D_{i50} (dB)**			
low	from 50–55	from 55–60	from 60–65	> 65
medium	from 55–60	from 60–65	from 65–70	> 70
high	from 60–65	from 65–70	from 70–75	> 75

SIA 181, Special uses 3.2.1.4, A.2.2.2

D Nomogram of necessary noise level correction ΔL$_{AS}$
depending on room volume V [m³] and common surface S [m³] of partition wall

SIA 181, E.2.1.2, Figure 10

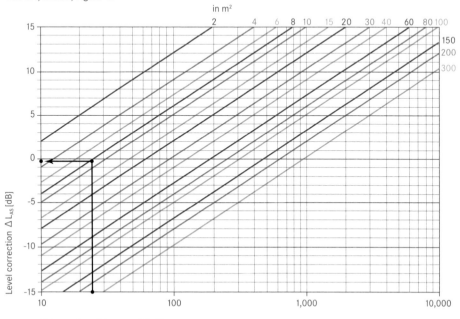

Room volume V = 25.2 m³
Common surface S = 8.4 m²
Necessary noise level correction ΔL$_{AS}$ ≥ -0.2 dB

E Volume related correction C$_V$ for airborne and impact sound

Volume V [m³]	Volume related correction C$_V$ [dB] or [dB(A)]
V < 200	0
200 ≤ V < 300	2
300 ≤ V < 500	3
500 ≤ V < 800	4
V ≥ 800	5

SIA 181, 2.4

DETERMINATION OF NOISE PROTECTION against impact sound
SIA 181

1. Determine sensitivity of receiving room
L_{RL} : required level: low – medium – high
see page 155

F 2. Determine noise source intensity of emitting room qualitatively
L_{NL} : noise level

G 3. Determine the required value for maximum acceptable standard impact sound level L'

4. Compute volume V of receiving room

H 5. Determine necessary noise level correction ΔL_{IS} from nomogram
or
$\Delta L_{IS} = 14.9 - 10 \log V$ (dB)

I Volume related correction C_v from table

6. Compute the maximum acceptable standard impact sound level $L'_{n,w}$
$L'_{n,w} + C_I \leq L' - \Delta L_{IS} - C_v$
$L'_{n,w}$: specific, depends on building component
C_I : spectral correction, depends on building part

7. Determine the assessed standard impact sound level
$L'_{n,w}$
$L'_{n,0,w}$ raw concrete floor slab
J $L'_{n,r,0,w}$ concrete reference floor slab without additional layer

8. Assessed reduction of impact sound level
$\Delta L_w = L'_{n,0,w} - (L'_{n,w} + C_I)$

K 9. The building component must have a value below the required standard impact sound level, through its construction, material thickness, or additional lagging.

Example: Living room above living room

Given:
Concrete floor slab with d = 20 cm between two living rooms, each with a volume of 80 m³

Sought:
Impact sound reduction ΔL_w to give the necessary protection from impact sound

1. Living room = receiving room
L_{RL} = medium

2. Living room = emitting room
L_{NL} = medium

3. Required value for floor slab L' = 53 dB

4. Receiving room V = 80 m³

5. Nomogram of noise level correction ΔL_{IS}
or
$\Delta L_{IS} = 14.9 - 10 \log 80 = -4.1$ (dB)

6. Corrected maximum acceptable standard impact sound level $L'_{n,w}$ of the floor slab
$L' - \Delta L_{IS} - C_v = 53 - (-4.1) - 0 = 57.1$ dB
$L'_{n,w} + C_I \leq 57.1$ dB

with volume related correction $C_v = 0$

7. Assessed standard impact sound level of raw concrete floor slab
$L'_{n,r,0,w} = 70.5$ dB

8. Assessed reduction of impact sound level
$\Delta L_w = L'_{n,r,0,w} - (L'_{n,w} + C_I)$
$\Delta L_w = 70.5 - 57.1 = 13.4$ dB

9. Select construction for impact sound reduction if necessary
see page 162
see SIA D 0189
see manufacturers' data

DIMENSIONING AGAINST IMPACT SOUND

If several rooms share the same floor/ceiling, dimensioning should be between the noisiest room above and the most sensitive room below.

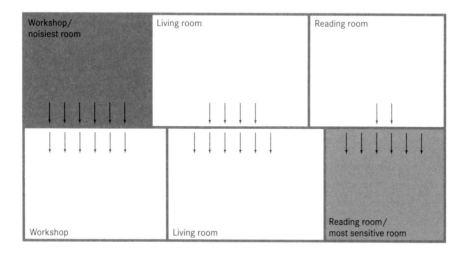

In many cases, impact sound is most relevant noise disturbance for the vertical sound transfer and is therefore the construction determining noise.

MINIMUM REQUIREMENTS FOR IMPACT SOUND

F	Noise source intensity	Low	Moderate	High	Very high
	Emitting room: examples	Reading room, waiting room, archive	Living room, bedroom, kitchen, bath, toilet, staircase, corridor, terrace, garage	Restaurant, school room, kindergarten, gym, workshop, music practice room	The same functions as under "high" including from 7 pm to 7 am
G	Noise sensitivity	Maximum acceptable standard impact sound level L'			
	low	63 dB	58 dB	53 dB	48 dB
	medium	58 dB	53 dB	48 dB	43 dB
	high	53 dB	48 dB	43 dB	38 dB

SIA 181, 3.2.2.2

H Nomogram of noise level correction ΔL$_{IS}$

SIA 181, E.3.1.2, Figure 12

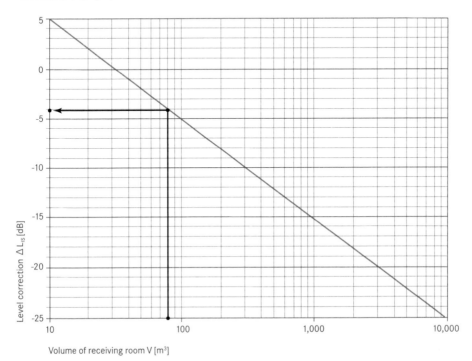

Volume of receiving room V [m³]

Room volume V = 80 m³
Necessary noise level correction ΔL$_{IS}$ ≥ -4.1

I Volume related correction C$_V$ for airborne and impact sound

Volume V [m³]	Volume correction C$_V$ [dB] or [dB(A)]
V < 200	0
200 ≤ V < 300	2
300 ≤ V < 500	3
500 ≤ V < 800	4
V ≥ 800	5

SIA 181, 2.4

J Raw concrete floor slab
Assessed standard impact sound level L'$_{n,r,0,w}$ [dB] without flooring
SIA 181, E.3.2.5, Figure 13

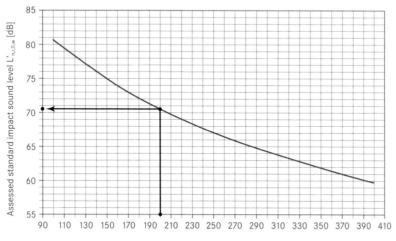

Concrete floor thickness d [mm]

Example
Concrete floor thickness 200 mm
Assessed standard impact sound level L'$_{n,r,0,w}$ = 70.5 dB

ASSESSED IMPACT SOUND REDUCTION ΔL_w [dB]

K Several flooring layers on a raw concrete floor slab

Additional flooring layers

Material	ΔL_w [dB]
Linoleum 2.5 mm	7
Linoleum on 2 mm cork	15
Linoleum on 5 mm porous wooden panels (380 kg/m²)	16
Cork linoleum 3.5 mm	15
Cork linoleum 7.0 mm	18
Cork parquet 6.0 mm	15
PVC flooring 1.5–2.0 mm	5
PVC flooring with 2 mm cork	14
PVC flooring with 3 mm felt layer, depending on execution	15–19
Rubber flooring 2.5 mm	10
Rubber flooring 5.0 mm, of which 4 mm porous rubber layer	24
Coco carpet	17–22
Carpets, depending on type	24–30
Needle felt flooring	17–22

Wooden flooring

Material	ΔL_w [dB]

Listel floors on wood

Directly mounted on floor	16
Mounted on 1 cm absorbing layer of rockwool or cork	24

Parquet flooring on

2.0 cm cork	6
0.7 cm bitumen felt	15
2 cm peat plates	16
1 cm porous wooden panels	16
1 cm porous wooden panels, on 0.5 cm mineral fibre panels	28

Floating screed floorings

Material	ΔL_w [dB]

Screed floorings of concrete with the following additional layers

Corrugated cardboard 0.3 cm	18
Porous wooden panels 1.2 cm	15
Polystyrene hard foam panels, 1 cm	26
Cork grit mats 0.6–0.8 cm	16
Cork grit mats 1.4 cm	22
Rubber grit mats	18
Coconut fibre mats 0.8 cm	23
Coconut fibre felt 1.3 cm	28
Mineral fibre panels 1.0 cm	27
Mineral fibre panels 1.5 cm	31
Mineral fibre felt 1.5 cm	31

Asphalt screed on

Porous wood fibre panels 2 cm	20
Cork grit mats 0.7 cm	19

DESIGN PRINCIPLES FOR NOISE PROTECTION

1. Noise suppression as close to the source as possible

2. The weakest element almost always determines the noise level impact
Compare: → Area ratios on buildings from approx. 1:2 to 1:10
Noise protection level differences of 20–60 dB, i.e. 1:10,000

3. De-coupling of adjacent elements, separated constructions:
→ Soft intermediate layers, joints if possible

4. Constructions with double layers are better than single-layer construction. Combine soft and hard bending materials.

5. Consider side transmissions → longitudinal conduction through neighbouring construction elements will bridge sound transmission even if very good sound isolation is put in place for the element itself.

6. Avoid stiff hard foam insulating materials (polystyrene, styrofoam etc.) on ceilings and walls → they can decrease the noise protection because of their stiffness.

7. When using construction systems always ask the supplier for a specific guarantee of the noise protection values.

8. Poor noise protection (lightweight construction, small mass) can be improved by increasing in noise absorption.

9. Indicate the required values in any invitation to tender.

Noise protection measure of composite building elements

$$R'_{res} = 10 \cdot \log \left(\frac{S_1 + S_2 + \dots}{S_1 \cdot 10^{-R_1/10} + S_2 \cdot 10^{-R_2/10} + \dots} \right)$$

$S_1, S_2,\dots$ = surfaces
$R_1, R_2,\dots$ = assessed standard impact sound level of the individual components

Airborne sound insulation of building elements

Interior walls

Light structures	34–45 dB
Two separated shells	50–55 dB
Single-shell massive walls	43–55 dB
Doors	17–40 dB

Exterior walls

Common massive walls, single layer	> 50 dB
Common massive walls, duoble layer	> 60 dB to > 70 dB
Light metal structures	< 40 dB
Exposed brickwork wall	up to 10 dB worse than plastered, because of joints
Stiff plastic foams	Diminishing sound isolation efficiency
Double/triple glazing	33–35 dB
Glazing with high sound insulation	< 48 dB
Box windows	< 60 dB

Noise level L_{res} of composite parts – example

Given: external noise level $L_e = 70$ dB

Wall	$A_{wa} = 10$ m^2	$R'_{wwa} = 50$ dB	$L_{iwa} = 20$ dB
Window	$A_{wi} = 4$ m^2	$R'_{wwi} = 40$ dB	$L_{iwi} = 30$ dB

Sought: resulting noise level L_{res}

$$I_{wa} = I_{ref} \cdot 10^{(0.1 \cdot L_{iwa})} \; \text{W/m}^2 = 10^{-12} \cdot 10^{(0.1 \cdot 20)} \; \text{W/m}^2 = 10^{-10} \; \text{W/m}^2$$

$$I_{wi} = I_{ref} \cdot 10^{(0.1 \cdot L_{iwi})} \; \text{W/m}^2 = 10^{-12} \cdot 10^{(0.1 \cdot 30)} \; \text{W/m}^2 = 10^{-9} \; \text{W/m}^2$$

$$I_{res} = \frac{A_{wi} \cdot I_{wi} + A_{wa} \cdot I_{wa}}{A_{wi} + A_{wa}} = \frac{4 \cdot 10^{-9} + 10 \cdot 10^{-10}}{4 + 10} = 3.57 \cdot 10^{-10}$$

$$L_{res} = 10 \log \left(\frac{I_{res}}{I_{ref}} \right) 10 \log \left(\frac{3.57 \cdot 10^{-10}}{10^{-12}} \right) = 26 \; \text{dB}$$

or directly

$$L_{res} = 10 \log \left(\frac{A_{wi} \cdot 10^{(0.1 \cdot L_{iwi})} + A_{wa} \cdot 10^{(0.1 \cdot L_{iwa})}}{A_{wi} + A_{wa}} \right) = 26 \; \text{dB}$$

A Noise transmission through a slab
Measures against resonant vibrations, choice of stiff or soft slabs

Material	Bending softness sufficient	Bending stiffness sufficient
Frequency	Resonance frequency $f_i > 1{,}600$ Hz → above the relevant frequency range	Limiting frequency $f_i < 200$ Hz → below the relevant frequency range
Thickness d	small	large
Bending wave speed c_{pl}	small	large

B Thickness of sufficiently soft or stiff materials

No.	Material	Bending softness sufficient ($f_i \geq 1{,}600$ Hz) Thickness less than [mm]	Bending stiffness sufficient ($f_i \geq 200$ Hz) Thickness more than [mm]
10	Heavy concrete		85
6	Light concrete, gypsum		150
3	Aerated concrete		220
8	Brick wall		115
4	Plasterboard	20	
4	Fibre concrete	10	
4	Hard fibre panel	19	
9	Plywood	13	
1	Soft fibre panel	45	
11	Glass, steel	7	
2	Lead	30	
5	Wood particle board	50	
7	Acrylic glass (PMMA)	20	

A Noise transmission through a slab

Measures against resonant vibrations, choice of stiff or soft slabs

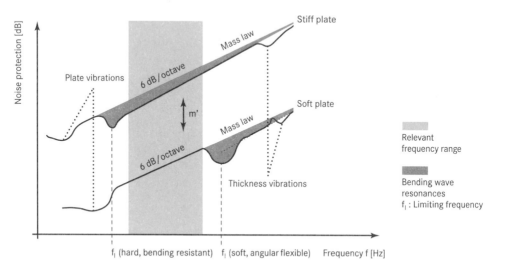

Relevant
frequency range

Bending wave
resonances
f_l : Limiting frequency

B Thickness of sufficiently soft and stiff materials

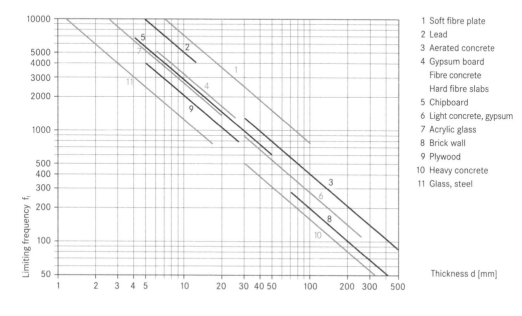

1 Soft fibre plate
2 Lead
3 Aerated concrete
4 Gypsum board
   Fibre concrete
   Hard fibre slabs
5 Chipboard
6 Light concrete, gypsum
7 Acrylic glass
8 Brick wall
9 Plywood
10 Heavy concrete
11 Glass, steel

RUNNING TIME – SOUND REFLECTIONS

A RUNNING TIME – SOUND REFLECTIONS
Determining the dimensions of performance spaces through the acceptable differences in sound path lengths.

DIRECT SOUND
on a direct path through the air

FIRST REFLECTIONS
on indirect paths by reflections from walls or ceiling

Time sequence of first reflections
Within a period of more than 20 milliseconds [ms], and up to 80–100 ms, the human ear adds the first reflections into a single sound impression, which it perceives as direct sound.

B PATH DIFFERENCES Δs [m]
Direct sound – first reflections
$\Delta s = v \cdot \Delta t$ [m]
Δs: Path difference [m]
v: Sound speed [m/s]
Δt: Time difference [m/s]

DIFFUSE SOUND
on even more indirect paths through several successive reflections from different surfaces

Reverberation time T [s]
The time it takes for a diffuse sound to die away

Short enough: so that sound continuation is not superimposed
Not too short: otherwise there will be no impression of space

A RUNNING TIME – SOUND REFLECTIONS

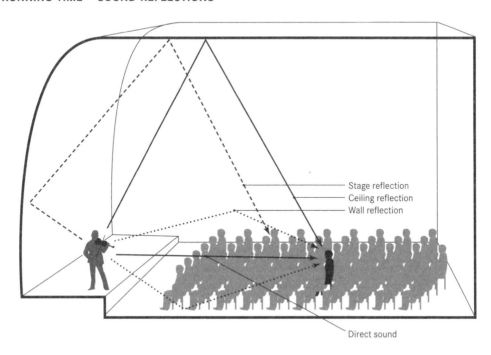

Stage reflection
Ceiling reflection
Wall reflection

Direct sound

B PATH DIFFERENCES Δs [m]
Direct sound – first reflections
Δt = 20 ms
v = 340 m/s → speed of sound (in air)
340 · 0.02 = 6.8 m

Sound detour	Delay	Effect
0.3–7 m	0.8–20 ms	Early interferences should be suppressed, as they colour the sound unpleasantly
7–17 m	20–50 ms	Range for speech
7–27 m	20–80 ms	Range for music
7–34 m	20–100 ms	Maximum range of accumulation by the ear
> 34 m	> 100 ms	Reflexions are perceived as disturbing echos

REVERBERATION TIME T [s]
after Sabine

Time required for the sound level to decrease by 60 dB after the sound source has been stopped
Decrease of the sound intensity by the factor 10^{-6}

$$T = 0.163 \cdot \frac{V}{A} \ [s]$$

0.163: Sabine's constant [s/m]
V: Room volume [m³]
A: Equivalent area of sound absorption [m²]
see page 174

$$A = \sum_{i=1}^{N} S_i \cdot a_i \ [m^2]$$

S_i: All surfaces of a room [m²]
a_i: Sound absorption factors of all existing surfaces/materials [–]
see page 175

C Desirable reverberation time T_{des} [s]

Reverberation times are longer if rooms are large rather than small, when their other properties remain the same
→ Volume V ~ d³, surfaces S ~ d²

Control of the reverberation time T

Reverberation time is shorter:
the more sound is reflected in the room, i.e.
the more complex the form of the inner room surface is,
the more these surfaces absorb sound

Best reverberation times –
rough dimensioning

Minimum room volume – volume figure K:
K > 4 m³ per person: speech
K > 6 m³ per person: chamber music
K > 8 m³ per person: symphonic music

Maximum room volume – V [m³]:
to be filled without electronic amplification
V < 3,000 m³ average speaker
V < 6,000 m³ experienced speaker
V < 10,000 m³ instrumental soloist
V < 25,000 m³ large symphony orchestra

C Desirable reverberation time T$_{des}$ [s]
at 500 Hz for music

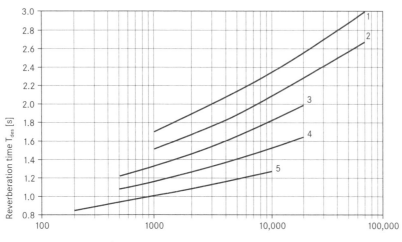

Room volume V [m³]

1 Rooms for symphonic music with chorus or organ music
2 Rooms for symphonic music
3 Rooms for solo and chamber music
4 Operas
5 Theatres, lecture halls

Best reverberation times T for different users

Room	Reverberation time T [s]
Office buildings	
Single office	0.6–1.0
Small office	0.6–0.8
Medium-sized office	0.6–0.8
Open-plan office	0.4–0.6
Data processing rooms	0.4–0.6
Canteens, recreation rooms	0.6–0.8
School buildings	
Classrooms	0.5–0.7
Classrooms, with singing	0.7–0.9
Music rooms	0.8–1.1
Music practice rooms	0.4–0.6
Dance hall	1.0–1.5
Classrooms for handicrafts	0.4–0.6
Assembly halls, auditoriums	0.9–1.2
Gyms, indoor swimming pools	1.0–1.5

Room	Reverberation time T [s]
Residential buildings	
Living and bedrooms	0.6–1.0
Hotels and restaurants	
Staircases	1.0–1.2
Corridors, halls	0.8–1.0
Guest rooms	0.8–1.2
Restaurants, bars	0.6–1.0
Radio and television studios	
Studio, 100–900 m²	max. 0.5–1.2
Rehearsal rooms	1.0–1.3
Broadcasting studios	0.5
Speakers' booths	max 0.3
Control rooms	0.5

Equivalent sound-absorbing surface A_k
Sound absorption by audience, chairs, musicians etc.
$\alpha_k = 1$; absorbing effect of a totally absorbent comparative surface S_k.

f [Hz]	125	250	500	1,000	2,000	4,000
Examples for S_k [m²]						
< 0.5 m² per person (choir)	0.15	0.25	0.40	0.50	0.60	0.60
approx. 0.65 m² per person (audience)	0.30	0.45	0.60	0.65	0.75	0.75
> 2 m² per person (musician)	0.45	0.65	0.85	1.00	1.10	1.10
Wooden chairs per seat, no covers	0.01	0.01	0.02	0.03	0.05	0.05
Folding chair, empty, wood	0.05	0.05	0.05	0.05	0.08	0.05
Person in church pew	0.25	0.34	0.41	0.45	0.45	0.38
Upholstered chair, empty, rubber foam	0.15	0.25	0.25	0.15	0.18	0.30
Person standing, or on wooden chair in large room	0.15	0.30	0.50	0.55	0.60	0.50
Child in classroom	0.12	0.18	0.26	0.32	0.38	0.38

Sound absorption factor a

Surface material	Octave mid-frequency					
	125	**250**	**500**	**1,000**	**2,000**	**4,000**
	Sound absorption factor a					
Absorber [1]	0.30	0.69	1.01	0.81	0.66	0.62
Acoustic panels, Flumroc	0.26	0.88	0.99	0.91	1.04	1.17
Acoustic panels, Heraklith	0.13	0.11	0.22	0.54	0.85	0.71
Concrete, gypsum, stucco, natural stone	0.02	0.02	0.03	0.04	0.05	0.05
Proscenium	0.40	0.40	0.60	0.70	0.80	0.80
Floorboard, parquet, wooden flooring (hollow, on battens)	0.10	0.08	0.06	0.05	0.05	0.05
Floorboard, parquet, chipboard (rigid supports)	0.03	0.04	0.04	0.05	0.05	0.05
Window, mirror	0.12	0.10	0.05	0.04	0.02	0.02
Chair, upholstered, unoccupied	0.45	0.60	0.70	0.80	0.80	0.80
Chair, wood, unoccupied	0.05	0.05	0.05	0.05	0.05	0.05
Lime plaster, wallpaper, gypsum plasterboard	0.02	0.03	0.04	0.05	0.06	0.08
Linoleum, PVC, rubber flooring	0.02	0.03	0.03	0.04	0.04	0.05
Linoleum, PVC, rubber flooring on felt layer	0.02	0.05	0.10	0.15	0.07	0.05
Marble, tile, clinker	0.01	0.01	0.02	0.02	0.02	0.03
Masonry, flat surface	0.02	0.03	0.03	0.04	0.05	0.07
Masonry, ribbed 10 mm	0.08	0.09	0.12	0.16	0.22	0.24
Metal ceiling, Gema	0.34	0.76	0.81	0.91	0.97	0.90
Masonite board, PAVATEX	0.37	0.30	0.48	0.71	0.88	0.89
Audience on wooden chairs	0.40	0.60	0.75	0.80	0.85	0.80
Audience on upholstered chairs	0.60	0.75	0.80	0.85	0.90	0.85
Foam-based wallpaper, approx. 8 mm	0.03	0.10	0.25	0.40	0.50	0.60
Carpet (PVC film on 5 mm felt)	0.02	0.09	0.20	0.15	0.07	0.05
Carpet, up to 5 mm thick	0.03	0.04	0.06	0.20	0.30	0.40
Carpet, more than 5 mm thick	0.03	0.06	0.10	0.30	0.50	0.60
Door (wood, varnished)	0.10	0.08	0.06	0.05	0.05	0.05
Curtains, ruched velvet	0.15	0.45	0.96	0.91	1.06	1.02

[1] Gypsum plasterboard, perforated (19.6% holes), lined with fibre felt and 3 cm mineral rockwool, 10 cm from wall

ACOUSTICAL DESIGN

A SOUND DISTRIBUTION

Acoustically important:
direction of the first reflections
Sound arriving from the side is heard better than
from above or behind; reflections from side walls
increase the spatial feeling of a performance
Reflections coming from the same direction as
the direct sound are less audible

Important for whole auditorium
Enough direct sound
Time relation (delay) between direct sound and
first reflections kept within appropriate limits
Sufficient sound impact from the side
Appropriate design of the room surfaces, side
walls, ceiling

Risk of fluttering echos
between parallel surfaces
Reflection of sound impulses back and forth
between parallel surfaces that absorb sound
poorly, exceeding the echo time limit of
80–100 ms.

Standing waves
Occur at distinct frequencies (wavelengths)
Frequency-selective effect as local resonances

B Constructive means of avoiding fluttering echos and standing waves
At least one side with increased absorption
factor a
Slight inclination or rotation of one surface
by approx. 5°

A SOUND DISTRIBUTION
Construction of sound beams using the mirror source method

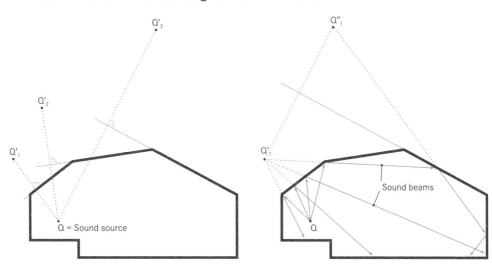

Q'₁: Source mirrored on first part of ceiling
Q'₂: Source mirrored on second part of ceiling
Q'₃: Source mirrored on third part of ceiling

B Constructive means of avoiding fluttering echos and standing waves

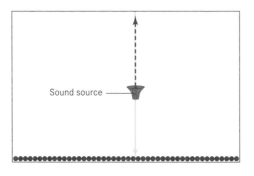

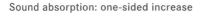

Sound absorption: one-sided increase

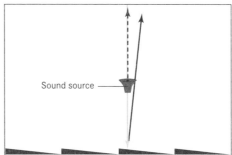

Sound reflection: inclination or rotation of one surface

ACOUSTICAL OPTIMIZATION OF INTERIOR SPACES

Example
Lecture hall:
Length 15 m
Width 9 m
Height 6 m
Audience 132 persons/seats

C Sound reflections in longitudinal section
in the central and rear part of auditorium:
Low density of sound beams
Poor sound supply
Danger of echos

Sound path difference > 17 m between direct sound and parts of the reflected sound beams
Risk of fluttering echos between stage and ceiling because of parallel surfaces

D Improvement with room shape – inclination of ceiling
Eliminates risk of echo
Improves reflection to the back of the auditorium – better distribution of sound

E Sound reflections in floor plan
Side wall reflections – oblique side walls, on the sides of the stage
Support of the sound supply to the central area

Reflections from the back wall
Reduced audibility in the front part
→ Improvement by inclining of the back wall, reflections to the rear areas
see illustration D

C Sound reflections in longitudinal section

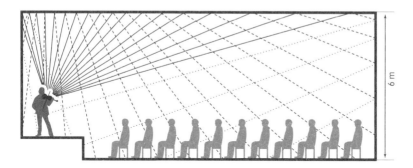

D Improvement with room shape – inclination of ceiling

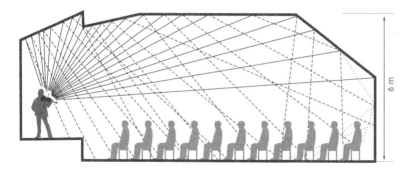

E Sound reflections in floor plan

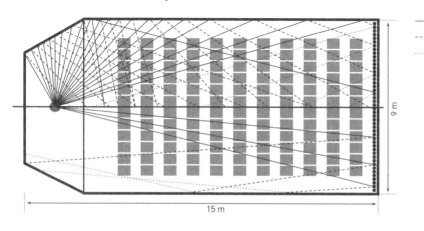

——— Direct sound
- - - - First reflection
· · · · · · Second reflection

SOUND REFLECTION
For higher standards, use additional reflectors
as separate surfaces, arranged appropriately

Redistribution of sound beams
Dilute in sound-rich zones
Condense in sound-poor zones

F Flat reflectors
Keep the existing divergence of the beams

G Convex reflectors
Diverge the sound beams

H Concave reflectors
Concentrate and focus the sound beams, may
produce disruptive effects

Diffuse reflectors (diffusors)
Undirected scattering, wide-ranging distribution of the sound beams, sound shower

Reflectors with structured surfaces
Effective only for wavelengths smaller than the
dimensions of the surface structures

Effect of reflectors
is stronger:
The greater the diameter compared to the
wavelength
The greater the space angle
The steeper the angle of the sound wave
incidence
The greater the mass of the reflector (area-
related mass)
Speech > 10 kg/m^2
Music > 40 kg/m^2

F Flat reflectors

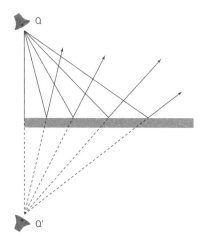

G Convex reflectors

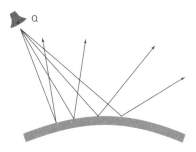

H Concave reflectors

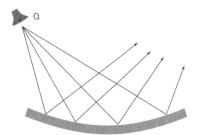

FREQUENCY RENDITION

CORRECTIVE ELEMENTS
Adjustment of the frequency rendition using frequency-dependent absorbers

A SOUND ABSORPTION
→ Reduces of reverberation time
→ Removes risk of echos
→ Corrects of frequency rendition

For high frequencies:
porous, open pored absorbers
Transform sound energy into heat by friction in a porous layer

Acoustic panels = porous absorbers
with high internal friction
e.g. chipboard with grooves and holes to increase surface area

Never paint surfaces of porous materials, as this will eliminate their effect

For medium frequencies:
panel absorber
A plywood, gypsum or similar board, mounted e.g. on battens so as not to hinder vibration, at a particular distance from the wall d_w [m]

The air behind the panel acts as a spring and the panel itself as vibrating mass with the resonant frequency f.

Porous, sound-absorbing materials in the hollow space behind the panels absorb sound particularly strongly at resonant frequency f and remove energy from the sound wave.

For low frequnecies:
Helmholtz resonators
Oscillators for high absorption at very low frequencies

Sound absorption factor a
→ for surfaces/materials
see table page 175

A SOUND ABSORPTION
Mounting of sound absorption surfaces

Sections

Ceiling plans

DESIGN PRINCIPLES FOR ACOUSTICAL PLANNING

PRIMARY STRUCTURE OF A ROOM

1. Volume index K [m³/person]

The maximum number of persons in an audience requires a minimum volume. Volume index K takes the reverberation time T roughly into account.

2. Maximum room volume V [m³]

Upper limit of the room volume for performances without electronic amplification Sound source strength is taken into account as well as the different lengths of the sound paths.

3. Sound distribution

First sketch of the space and its internal form. This determines lateral sound and first reflections

4. Sound distribution

Draw some sound beams to check the effect of the space's form on its sound distribution capacities.

see mirrored source method page 177

5. Sound distribution

Adapt the room shape if the sound distribution is uneven.

SECONDARY STRUCTURE

6. Application of reflectors

In the case of parallel walls and to avoid fluttering echos, or to correct unfavourable sound waves in a given room shape, sound reflectors are applied.

7. Determination of the existing absorption a

see pages 174–175
see manufacturers' data

8. Check of the expected reverberation time

by computation

9. Comparison between required and expected value of reverberation time

Computation of extra need of sound absorbing surfaces

FREQUENCY SPECIFIC MEASURES

10. Identification and adaptation

of the frequency rendition by specific absorbers

DAYLIGHT

CHARACTERISTIC VALUES FOR LIGHTING

A LIGHT – SENSITIVITY CURVE OF THE HUMAN EYE

Electromagnetic waves with wavelengths λ of between 380 and 780 nanometres [nm].
The maximum sensitivity of the human eye is at 555 nm in the yellow-green range.

LUMINOUS FLUX Φ [lm]

$\Phi = K \cdot P$ [lm]

Total amount of light a source emits per unit of time
K: Radiation equivalent of the light source [lm/W]
P: Power of the light source in watts [W]

RADIATION EQUIVALENT K [lm/W]

The energy flux of the light source is weighted according to the sensitivity of the eye, which is dependent on the wavelength λ, by a conversion factor K:
Radiation equivalent K in lumens per watt [lm/W]

Daylight

K = 90–100 lm/W

Incandescent light bulb

K = approx. 14 lm/W

Maximum radiation equivalent K

Monochromatic light of Na-vapour lamps:
λ = 589 nm
K = 673 lm/W

A LIGHT – SENSITIVITY CURVE OF THE HUMAN EYE

Spectral sensitivity V [λ] and V' [λ] of the human eye at wavelength λ

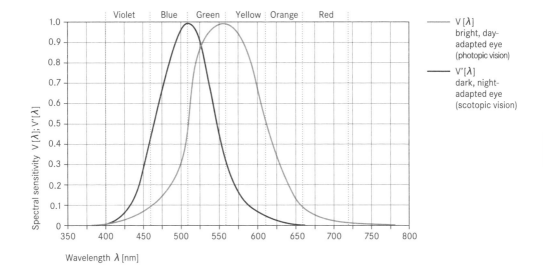

λ = 555 nm: Maximum sensitivity of the human eye (day adapted)

LUMINOUS INTENSITY I [cd=lm/sr]
(LUMINOSITY)

$$I = \frac{\Phi}{\Omega} \text{ [cd = lm/sr]}$$

Amount of light emitted, for solid angle Ω
in candelas [cd]
Sphere: 4π
Hemisphere: 2π

Solid angle $\Omega \cong \dfrac{A}{r^2}$ [sr] (steradians)

A: Surface of the cap of the sphere [m²]
r: Radius of the sphere [m]

LUMINANCE L [cd/m² = lm/m²sr]

$$L = \frac{I}{A} = \frac{\Phi}{A \cdot \Omega} \text{ [cd/m}^2 = \text{lm/m}^2\text{sr]}$$

A: Luminous surface [m²]
Ω: Solid angle [sr]

Differences in luminance are relevant for visual
perception

ILLUMINANCE E [lx=lm/m²]

$$E = \frac{\Phi}{A} \text{ [lx = lm/m}^2\text{]}$$

A: Illuminated area [m²]
Effect on the illuminated object. Luminous flux
in relation to the size of the illuminated surface
in lux [lx].

SECONDARY LIGHT SOURCE L
[cd/m² =lm/m²sr]

$$L = \frac{E \cdot R}{\pi} \text{ [cd/m}^2 = \text{lm/m}^2\text{sr]}$$

Any illuminated surface with diffuse reflectivity
R represents a secondary light source with a
luminance L:
indirect illumination/glare
e.g. matt white writing paper (R = 0.8) in full sun

CHARACTERISTIC VALUES OF LIGHTING – INTERRELATIONSHIPS

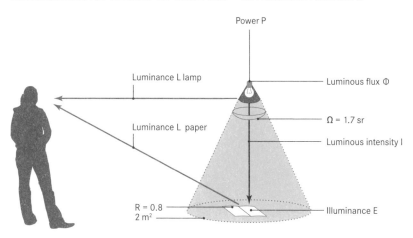

Example:

Luminous flux Φ
1,000 lm

Luminous intensity I
I = 1,000 lm: 1.7 sr = 588.2 lm/sr = 588.2 cd

Luminance L of a lamp
L = 588.2 cd: 0.01 m² = 58,850 cd/m²

Illuminance E
E = 1,000 lm: 2 m² = 500 lx = 500 lm/m²

Luminance L of paper (secondary light source)
L = 500 lx · 0.8/π = 127.3 cd/m² = 127.3 lm/m²sr

ILLUMINANCE E [lx] OUTDOORS

Illuminance	E [lx]
Direct solar radiation	60,000–100,000
Dull summer's day	20,000
Low stratus, in winter	10,000
Dull winter's day	3,000
Night with full moon	0.25
New moon, starlight	0.01

100 lux correspond to 1 W/m² solar irradiation.

REQUIRED ILLUMINANCE E [lx]

Minimum requirement for luminance
L > 200 [cd/m²]
Reflectivity R, e.g. R = 0.8

$$E = \frac{L \cdot \pi}{R} = \frac{200 \cdot 3.14}{0.8} = 785 \text{ lx}$$

Demanding visual tasks
Illuminance E of 500–1,000 lx recommended

**Guidelines for illuminance E
according to visual task**

Level	E [lx]	Visual task
1	20	
2	50	Orientation, momentary stay
3	100	
4	200	Light visual task, large details, strong contrast
5	300	
6	500	Normal visual task, medium details, medium contrast
7	750	
8	1,000	Difficult visual task, small details, low contrast
9	1,500	Very difficult visual task, very small details, very low contrast
10	2,000	

A VISUAL PERCEPTION

Increases strongly with the luminance L of the environment,
Flattens below 100 cd/m^2
Good visual perception:
Adaption luminance L_a with maximum of between 200 and 2000 cd/m^2

LUMINANCE L – MEAN VALUES

Examples	Luminance L [cd/m²]
Sun at zenith	up to 1.6×10^9
Sun at horizon	approx. 6,000,000
Clear sky, on average	8,000
Covered sky	3,500
Moon	2,500
Candle flame	7,000
Acetylene flame	100,000
Fluorescent tube	3,000–13,000
Incandescent lamp	200–500
Light bulb, opal	10,000–50,000
Light bulb, matt	50,000–500,000
Light bulb, clear	$10^6 – 20 \times 10^6$
Halogen lamp	$8 \times 10^6 – 16 \times 10^6$
Torch	$160 \times 10^6 – 400 \times 10^6$
Na-vapour lamps, low pressure, clear	$1.9 \times 10^6 – 6.2 \times 10^6$
Hg-vapour lamps with fluorescence	40,000–250,000
Hg-vapour lamps, high pressure	up to 1.7×10^9
Xenon lamps, high pressure	$150 \times 10^6 – 950 \times 10^6$
Well-lit streets	2
Writing paper in well-lit office	250 (at 1000 lx)
Lower limit for visual perception	10^{-5}

A VISUAL PERCEPTION

Adaption luminance L_a with maximum of between 200 and 2,000 cd/m²

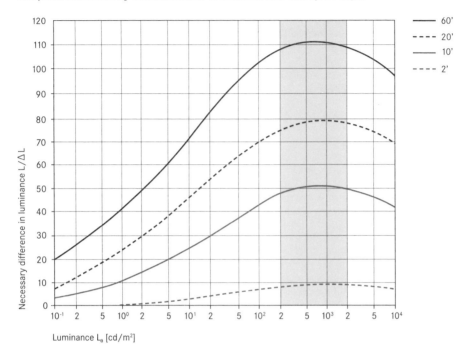

Luminance L_a [cd/m²]

Necessary difference in luminance ΔL for good visual perception, depending on adaption luminance L_a:
Sensitivity to differences for four objects of different size: 2' to 60'
Object size in viewing angles, defining space between between them, e.g. two points/lines

Quotient $L/\Delta L$ for good visual perception:
smaller – ΔL to luminance L must be greater for smaller objects (2')
larger – ΔL to luminance L can be smaller for larger objects (60')

DAYLIGHT TRANSMISSION FACTOR τ_v [–]

The daylight transmission of glazing is weighted with the sensitivity of the human eye:
High values for good daylight supply
Reduce transmission to avoid overheating: selective coatings

Lower acceptance limit for transmission (reduction of view to the outside)
Daylight transmission
→ minimum: $\tau_v \geq 0.2 = 20\%$

Avoidance of glare
Daylight transmission
→ maximum: $\tau_v \leq 0.1 = 10\%$

Daylight transmission τ_v of below 10% can avoid glare but yields insufficient daylight level
→ need for variable sun shading

ENERGY IMPORTANCE OF DAYLIGHT

Better daylight supply can influence the light conditions of interiors for approximately 50–65% of the working hours of a year of approximately 2,000 h

Magnitude of energetic relevance
Daylight – artificial light – low-energy building

Artifical lighting of 12 W/m²,
1,000 h influenceable
12,000 Wh/m²a = 12 kWh/m²a
→ 12 kWh/m² · 3,600 s = 43 MJ/m²a

For comparison:
→ Energy need of low-energy buildings
100–150 MJ/m²a

LUMINANCE DISTRIBUTION OF THE SKY

The CIE standard sky shows the relationship of luminance:
Zenith: horizon = 3 : 1

Completely, evenly covered sky:

$$L_a = \frac{L_{90}}{3}(1 + 2 \cdot \sin a)$$

L_a: Luminance at elevation a [cd/m²]
L_{90}: Luminance at zenith [cd/m²]

Ratio of illuminance E_v on a vertical plane to illuminance E_h on a horizontal plane:

$$\frac{E_v}{E_h} = 0.397$$

Illuminance E_v on vertical glazing is thus less than 40% of illuminance E_h on horizontal glazing.
compare daylight quotient DF

INFLUENCE OF SHADOWING
on vertical and horizontal planes
Zenith/high: small range for angle but high intensity
Horizon/low: large range for angle but low intensity

Standard daylight integration

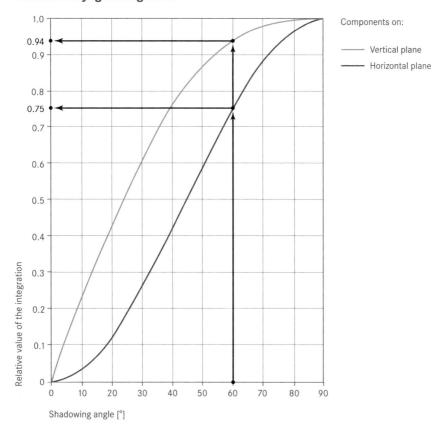

Components on:

——— Vertical plane
——— Horizontal plane

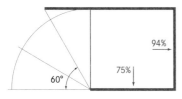

Example
A horizontal shadow with a shadow angle of 60°
reduces the intensity on a horizontal plane to 75%
and on a vertical plane to 94% of the total luminous
flux of an evenly covered sky.

DAYLIGHT FACTOR DF

$$DF = \frac{E_1}{E_0} \cdot 100 \ [\%]$$

Ratio of the horizontal indoor illuminance E_1 at a given room-point P to the simultaneous outdoor illuminance E_0 from an unobstructed, regularly overcast sky; according to CIE standard sky.

COMPONENTS OF THE DAYLIGHT FACTOR [%]

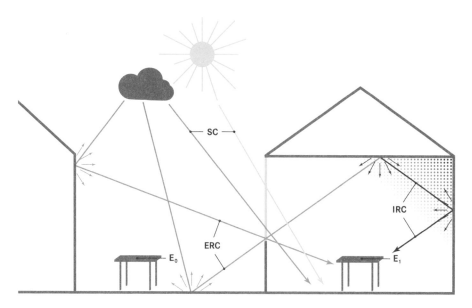

SC: Sky component, direct light from the sky
ERC: Externally reflected component, light reflected from opposing exterior surfaces
IRC: Internally reflected component, light reflected from internal surfaces
E_0: External horizontal illuminance
E_1: Internal horizontal illuminance

DETERMINATION OF THE DAYLIGHT FACTOR [%]

$$DF = \tau_v \cdot K_1 \cdot K_2 \cdot (SC + ERC + IRC) \; [\%]$$

where

$\tau_v =$
Daylight transmission factor of the glazing [–]

$K_1 =$
Reduction factor for the amount of framing [–]
0.7–0.9, depending on frame type
$K_1 = 1 - A_{frame}/A_{window}$

$K_2 =$
Reduction factor for dirt, pollution on glazing [–]
0.5–0.85, depending on cleaning and exposure

0. Geometry of a room

Draw the window openings and any obstacles, e.g. neighbouring houses visible in the window opening.

Mark the horizontal and vertical angles into the Waldram diagram.

1. Sky component SC, direct light

$$SC = n_{dl} \cdot 0.05$$

Count the number of squares n_{dl} in the window opening of the Waldram diagram:
Window opening minus any obstructions

2. Externally reflected component ERC

$$ERC = n_{ob} \cdot 0.05 \cdot \rho$$

Obstructions:
Count the number of squares n_{ob} of the obstructions in the Waldram diagram
Reflectivity of the obstructions:
Assumed mean value $\rho = 0.15$, otherwise use tables

3. Internally reflected component IRC [%]

$$IRC = \frac{A_{wi}}{A_R} \cdot \frac{1}{(1-\rho_m)} \cdot (f_u \cdot \rho_{fw} + f_d \cdot \rho_{cw}) \cdot 100 \; [\%]$$

as a function of

A A_{wi}/A_R
Ratio of the glazing/window area A_{wi} to the total internal surface of the room A_R

**Mean reflectivity ρ_m
of all internal surfaces**

**B Mean reflectivity ρ_{fw}
lower part of a room**
below the horizontal plane across the middle of the glazing height, without window wall

**C Mean reflectivity ρ_{cw}
upper part of a room**
above the horizontal plane across the middle of the glazing height, without window wall

D Obstruction distance angle a
measured from the centre of the glazing

→ **Window factors f_u, f_d**
f_u: Contribution of the reflection on the floor, upwards
f_d: Contribution of the reflection on the ceiling, downwards
f_u and f_d depend on obstruction distance angle a
→ from diagram
see page 203

A A$_{wi}$/A$_R$ and ρ_m

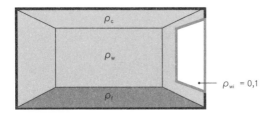

ρ_{wi} = 0,1

ρ_c: Reflectivity of the ceiling
ρ_w: Reflectivity of the wall
ρ_f: Reflectivity of the floor
ρ_{wi}: Reflectivity of the window

Standard values:
Ceiling 80–90%
Walls 40–60%
Floor 20–40%

B Mean reflectivity ρ_{fw} lower part of a room

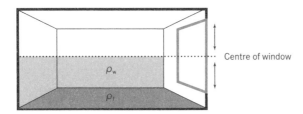

Centre of window

C Mean reflectivity ρ_{cw} upper part of a room

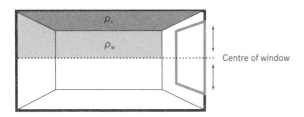

Centre of window

D Obstruction distance angle a and window factors f$_u$, f$_d$

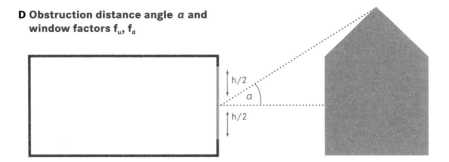

h/2

a

h/2

Waldram diagram

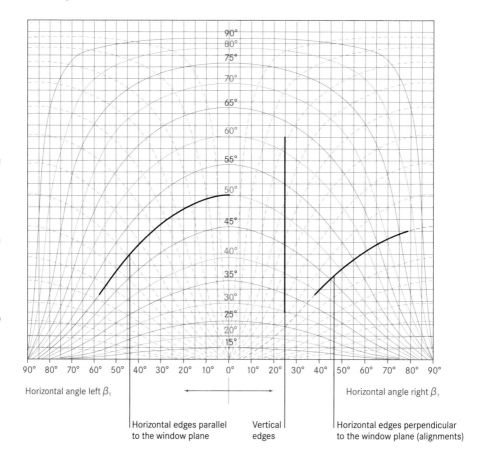

Vertical angles ε: for window ε_wi and obstruction ε_ob

Horizontal angle left β_l

Horizontal angle right β_r

Horizontal edges parallel
to the window plane

Vertical
edges

Horizontal edges perpendicular
to the window plane (alignments)

Window factors f_u and f_d at obstruction distance angle a

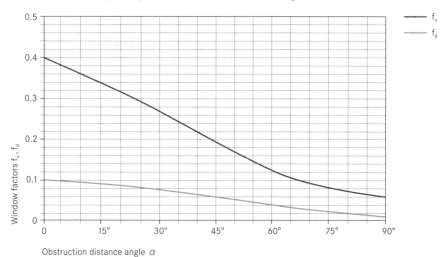

Obstruction distance angle a

Reflectivities ρ

Materials		Coat of paint		Natural materials	
Maple, birch	approx. 0.6	white	0.75–0.85	Soil, earth, humid	approx. 0.07
Oak, light, polished	0.25–0.35	light grey	0.4–0.6	Grass, dark green	0.04–0.06
Oak, dark, polished	0.1–0.15	medium grey	0.25–0.35	Vegetation, average	0.25–0.35
Chipboard, cream colour	0.5–0.6	light blue	0.4–0.5	New snow	0.75
Granite	0.2–0.25	dark blue	0.15–0.2	Old snow	0.65
Sandstone	0.2–0.4	light green	0.45–0.55	Skin, untanned	approx. 0.45
Limestone	0.35–0.55	dark green	0.15–0.2	Velvet, black	0.005–0.04
Marble, polished	0.3–0.7	light yellow	0.6–0.7		
Mortar, light, lime plaster	0.4–0.45	brown	0.2–0.3		
Gypsum plaster	approx. 0.8	pink	0.45–0.55		
Plywood, raw	0.25–0.4	dark red	0.15–0.2		
Cement, concrete, raw	0.2–0.3				
Bricks, tile red, new	0.1–0.15				

DF COMPUTATION Example

E 0. Geometry of the room
see drawings

Horizontal angles
$\beta_{wil} = 20°$
$\beta_{wir} = 35°$
$\beta_{or1} = 10°$
$\beta_{or2} = 15°$

Vertical angles
$\varepsilon_{ob} = 35°$
$\varepsilon_{wi} = 40°$

Surfaces
Walls: 56.1 m²
(2 x 4.3 x 2.7) + (2 x 6.1 x 2.7)
minus windows: 3.8 m²
(2.4 x 1.6)
Floor: 26.2 m² (4.3 x 6.1)
Ceiling: 26.2 m² (4.3 x 6.1)
Total A_R: 104.7 m²
Window A_{wi}: 3.8 m² (2.4 x 1.6)
Total: 108.5 m²

Reflectivities ρ
Wall: $\rho_w = 0.9$
Floor: $\rho_f = 0.5$
Ceiling: $\rho_c = 0.8$
Windows: $\rho_{wi} = 0.1$
Obstruction: $\rho = 0.15$

F Waldram diagram, counting n_{dl}, n_{ob}
$n_{dl} \cong 61$ squares
$n_{ob} \cong 28$ squares
see page 206

1. Sky component SC, direct light
$SC = 0.05 \cdot 61 = 3.05$

2. Externally reflected component ERC
$ERC = 0.05 \cdot 28 \cdot 0.15 = 0.21$

3. Internally reflected component IRC
$A_{wi}/A_R = 3.8/104.7 = 0.036$
$\rho_m = (0.9 \cdot 52.3 + 0.5 \cdot 26.2 + 0.8 \cdot 26.2 + 0.1 \cdot 3.8)/108.5 = 0.75$
$\rho_{fw} = (0.9 \cdot 24.75 + 0.5 \cdot 26.2)/51.0 = 0.69$
$\rho_{cw} = (0.9 \cdot 19.8 + 0.8 \cdot 26.2)/46.0 = 0.84$

Obstruction distance angle a
$a = 45° \rightarrow$ window factors

$\rightarrow$ Read off f_u and f_d from diagram "window factors"
$f_u = 0.19$
$f_d = 0.06$
see page 207

Internally reflected light IRC
$IRC = 0.036 \cdot 1/0.75 \cdot (0.19 \cdot 0.69 + 0.06 \cdot 0.84) \cdot 100 = 0.86\%$

4. Daylight transmission factor of glazing
$\tau_v = 0.8$

5. Reduction factors
Framing $K_1 = 0.85$
Dirt, pollution on glazing $K_2 = 0.75$

6. Daylight factor
$DF = (SC + ERC + IRC) \cdot \tau_v \cdot K_1 \cdot K_2$
$DF = (3.05 + 0.21 + 0.86) \cdot 0.8 \cdot 0.85 \cdot 0.75 = 2.1\%$

E 0. Geometry of the room

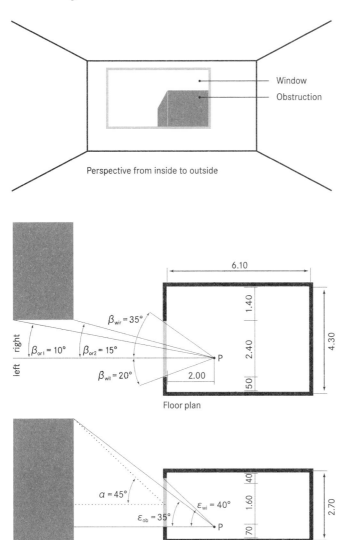

Perspective from inside to outside

Floor plan

Section

P: Position P inside for determining DF
Illustrations not to scale

F Waldram diagram

Mark window and obstruction of opposing exterior surfaces

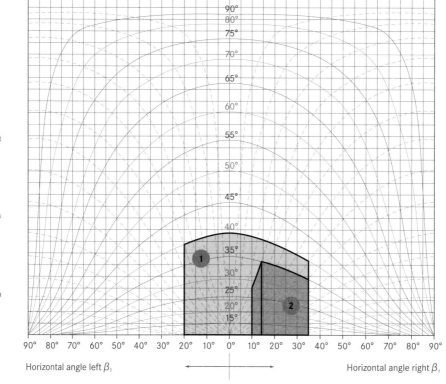

Counting n_{dl}, n_{ob}
1 $n_{dl} \cong 61$ squares
2 $n_{ob} \cong 28$ squares

Window factors f_d and f_u

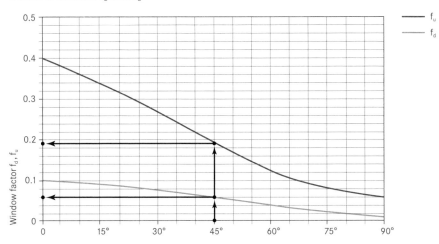

Obstruction distance angle α

Example

$\alpha = 45°$

$\rightarrow f_u = 0.19$

$\rightarrow f_d = 0.06$

EFFECT AND AVAILABILITY OF DAYLIGHT

Goals
Ensure physical and psychological comfort
Save electrical energy by reducing the use of artificial lighting
Reduce cooling load

Availability
Covered, cloudy sky is the most common state in many countries.
Daylight thus makes a limited contribution to reducing artificial lighting.

A Reducing artificial lighting by using daylight
The curves for N, S, E, W show:

with $f \cdot \tau_v = 0.15-0.25$ the potential for reducing artificial lighting is fully exploited, and is limited to about 35%.
f: Glazed proportion of facade [-]
τ_v: Daylight transmission factor [-]

B Percentages of operating times using daylight alone, for different daylight factors DF and required illuminances E

For any lighting requirement, based on the frequency distribution of the available daylight intensities and of the daily working time
Winter: 07.00–17.00 CEST
Summer: 08.00–18.00 CEST

Contribution of daylight
The contribution depends mainly on the proportion of glazing f [%] and its daylight transmission factor τ_v.

Example
For required illuminance E of 500 lx, daylight with a DF of
2%: never covers the need
5%: covers it up to 50%
12%: covers it up to 83%

Savings with installed artificial lighting with optimum control of approx. 12 W/m^2 and 2,000 h working hours per year:
2%: none
5%: approx. 12 kWh/m^{2}a – corresponds to CHF 2.20/m^{2}a
12%: approx. 20 kWh/m^{2}a – corresponds to CHF 3.60/m^{2}a
(1 kW/h at CHF 0.18; 2007)

An improvment from 2% to 5% yields savings of about CHF 2.20/m^{2}a.

The relation is not linear and has a lower limit, which, for an illuminance E of 500 lx, is at a DF of about 3%.
The use of sun shading and the resulting reduction of the DF is not taken into account.

A Reducing artificial lighting by using daylight

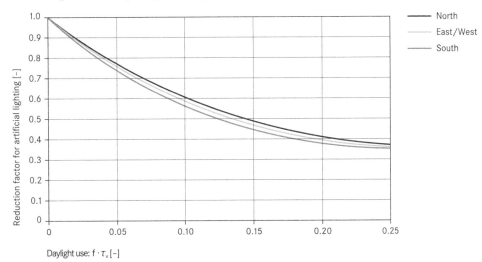

Reduction factor for artificial lighting [–]

Daylight use: $f \cdot \tau_v$ [–]

— North
— East/West
— South

**B Percentages of operating times with daylight only
for different DFs and required illuminances E given**

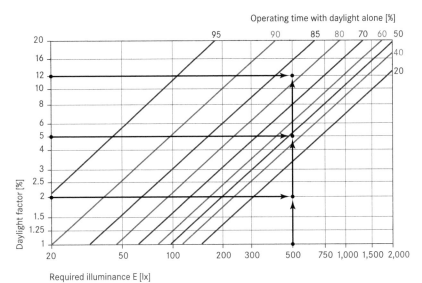

Operating time with daylight alone [%]

Daylight factor [%]

Required illuminance E [lx]

DESIGN PRINCIPLES FOR GOOD DAYLIGHTING

1. The maximum luminous flux Φ available for a room with lateral daylight impact is a function of the room height and the facade openings.

2. The ratio between room height and room depth essentially determines the daylight supply.

3. Without additional measures and at standard room height, daylight is useful up to about 6 m from the window.

4. The higher the windows are situated in the external wall, the better their daylight effect. The lintel should be kept as small as possible.

5. Parts of a window below desk height do not contribute much to daylighting, but the impact of their extra surfaces can increase heating or cooling load.

6. The internal surfaces should be kept as bright as possible. Relative to the contrast requirements, the following reflectivities are recommended:
Ceiling: 80–90%
Walls: 40–60%
Machines and apparatus: 25–45%
Floor: 20–40%

7. Low obstructions do not influence daylighting near the windows, but do have an influence in the depth of the room.

8. Skylights are a particularly efficient source of daylight. Sunshades should be considered to protect from thermal radiation, to prevent overheating in summer.

9. Fixed, shadow-casting elements such as brises-soleil, balconies etc. reduce the mean DF. see graph on page 197
Principally they have an effect on the horizontal daylight component and therefore on the direct light from the sky, i.e. on the DF near the window.
The effect on the vertical daylight component, and therefore in the depth of the room, is much smaller.
This reduces the difference between the DF near the window and in the depth of the room.

10. Glazed atria generally have no positive effect on daylighting of the nearby rooms:
The high obstruction angle with a ratio of about 2:3 eliminates a large part of the vertical daylight component, especially in the depth of the room.
The glazed roof further reduces the horizontal component because of dirt on the glazing and the loadbearing structure of the roof.

Daylight factor
at different room depths and positions of external, white louvre blinds

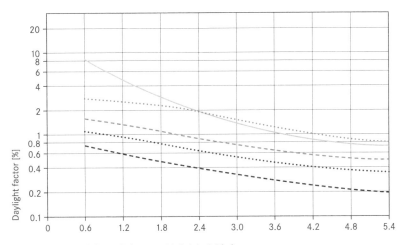

Room depth from window, at table height 0.7 [m]

———— Window with sun protection glazing, τ_v approx. 40%, without louvre blinds

· · · · · · · Window with white louvre blinds, position 0° (horizontal)

– – – – Window with white louvre blinds, position 30°

· · · · · · · Window with white louvre blinds, position 45°

– – – – Window with white louvre blinds, position 60°

Emotional effect of natural lighting

Level	Daylight factor	Effect	Internal lightness	Impression, mood
I	< 1 1–2	low	dark to dim	calming separated from the outside self-contained
II	2–4 4–7	medium to high	dim to bright	better gradual connection to the outside
III	7–12 > 12	high to very high	bright to very bright	stimulating open connected to the outside

GREEK ALPHABET

Greek letters

A	α	Alpha
B	β	Beta
Γ	γ	Gamma
Δ	δ	Delta
E	ε	Epsilon
Z	ζ	Zeta
H	η	Eta
Θ	θ	Theta
I	ι	Iota
K	κ	Kappa
Λ	λ	Lambda
M	μ	Mu
N	ν	Nu
Ξ	ξ	Xi
O	o	Omicron
Π	π	Pi
P	ρ	Rho
Σ	σ	Sigma
T	τ	Tau
Υ	υ	Upsilon
Φ	φ	Phi
X	χ	Chi
Ψ	ψ	Psi
Ω	ω	Omega

SYMBOLS AND UNITS

Factors and their denominations

10^{-15}	f	femto
10^{-12}	p	pico
10^{-9}	n	nano
10^{-6}	µ	micro
10^{-3}	m	milli
10^{3}	k	kilo
10^{6}	M	mega
10^{9}	G	giga
10^{12}	T	tera
10^{15}	P	peta
10^{18}	E	exa

Conversion of Imperial units

Length	inch	1 in = 2.54 cm
	foot	1 ft = 12 in = 0.3048 m
	yard	1 yd = 3 ft = 0.9144 m
	mile	1 mile = 1,760 yd = 1,609 m
Area	square foot	1 ft^2 = 0.0929 m^2
Mass	ounce	1 oz = 28.3495 g
	pound	1 lb = 16 oz = 0.4536 kg
Energy	Btu, British thermal unit	1 Btu = 1.05506 kJ
Power	Btu/h	1 Btu/h = 0.293 W
Thermal conductivity	Btu/h·ft	Btu/h·ft = 1.7306 W/mK
Heat flux density	Btu/h·ft^2	1 Btu/h·ft^2 = 3.155 W/m^2
Heat transfer coefficient	Btu/h·ft^2·F	Btu/h·ft^2·F = 5.674 W/m^{2}K
velocity	fpm, feet per minute	ft/min = 0.00508 m/s
air flow	cfm, cubic feet per minute	1 ft^3/min = 0.4719 lt/s
moisture	gr/lb, grain per pound	gr/lb = 0.143 g/kg
pressure	lb/ ft^2, pound per square foot	lb/ ft^2 = 47.9 Pa
Temperature	Fahrenheit	°F = 1.8 · °C + 32 °C = (°F − 32) · 5/9

Work, energy, heat quantity

	J (= N x m)	MJ	kWh	kcal	Btu
J (= N x m)	1	10^{-6}	0.278×10^{-6}	0.239×10^{-3}	0.9478134×10^{-3}
MJ	10^6	1	0.278	238.663	0.9478134×10^3
kWh	3.6×10^6	3.6	1	862	3,412.128
kcal	4.19×10^3	4.19×10^{-3}	1.16×10^{-3}	1	3.968305
Btu	1.05506×10^3	1.00506×10^{-3}	0.0002930722	0.2519968	1

Power, heat flow

	W (= J/s)	kW	PS	kcal/h	Btu/h
W (= J/s)	1	10^{-3}	1.36×10^{-3}	0.860	3.413
kW	10^3	1	1.36	860	$3.413.10^3$
PS	0.735×10^3	0.735	1	632	$0.398.10^{-3}$
kcal/h	1.16	1.16×10^{-3}	1.5×10^{-3}	1	0.253
Btu/h	0.293	$10^{-3} \times 0.293$	$2.508.10^3$	3.959	1

Water vapour conductivity

	mg/mhPa	kg/msPa	g/mhTorr
mg/mhPa	1	0.278×10^{-9}	0.133
kg/msPa	7.5	2.08×10^{-9}	1
g/mhTorr	3.6×10^9	1	0.48×10^9

Pressure, mechanical tension

	Pa = N/m² = kg/ms²	bar	mm WS (= 10^{-4}at)	Torr (mm Hg)
Pa = N/m² = kg/ms²	1	10^{-5}	0.102	750×10^{-5}
bar	10^5	1	0.102×10^5	750
mm WS (= 10^{-4}at)	9.81	9.81×10^{-5}	1	736×10^4
Torr (mm Hg)	133	133×10^{-5}	13.6	1

PHYSICAL QUANTITIES

In principle, the internationally valid SI units and abbreviations are used.
Other terms used by the SIA etc. are listed in brackets.

Name	Description	Equation	Symbol	Units
Length, width, height, depth			l, w, h, d	m (metre) (mm = 10^{-3} m)
Area		$l \cdot w$	A	m²
Volume		$l \cdot w \cdot h$	V	m³
Mass			m	kg (g, tons)
Density (bulk density, gross density)	Mass per volume	$\rho = m/V$	ρ	kg/m³
Force			F	N (newton = mkg/s²)
Heat (energy)			Q	J (joule = Nm), kJ, MJ
Power			P, $\dot{Q}$	W (watt = J/s), kW, MW
Pressure	Force per unit area	$p = F/A$	p	Pa (pascal = N/m²), 1 bar = 100,000 Pa
Temperature			θ, T	K (kelvin) °C (degree celsius)
Heat conductivity	Material property	$\lambda = \dot{Q} \cdot d/A \cdot \Delta\theta$	λ	W/mK
Specific heat capacity	Material property	$c = Q/m \cdot \Delta\theta$	c	J/kgK
Absolute humidity	Partial pressure of water vapour		p	Pa
	Saturation pressure of water vapour		p_{sat}	Pa
	Water vapour content of air		v	g/m³
	Water vapour content of saturated air		v_{sat}	g/m³
Relative humidity of air	Existing absolute humidity in relation to humidity at saturation	$\varphi = p/p_{sat}$ $\varphi = v/v_{sat}$	φ	given in %
Moisture content of materials	Water content per unit	m_w/m	f	g/kg; g/m³

QUANTITY EQUIVALENTS OF ENERGY SOURCES
without consideration of efficiency

Unit	Energy source	MJ	kg	kg	l	kg	m³	m³	kWh	kg	kg	kg
			Coal	Fuel oil EL H$_o$	Fuel oil EL H$_u$	Liquid gas (propane, butane)	Natural gas H$_o$ (Zurich)	Natural gas H$_u$ (Zurich)	Electricity	Wood (air-dried)	Wood chips	Wood pellets
1 kg	Coal	29.3	1.00	0.69	0.82	0.64	0.78	0.87	8.14	1.89	2.42	1.63
1 kg	Fuel oil EL H$_o$	38.1	1.30	1.00	1.06	0.82	0.89	1.12	10.56	2.36	3.15	2.11
1 l	Fuel oil EL H$_u$	35.9	1.23	0.84	1.00	0.78	0.95	1.06	9.97	2.32	2.97	1.99
1 kg	Liquid gas (propane, butane)	46.0	1.57	1.08	1.28	1.00	1.22	1.36	12.78	2.97	3.80	2.56
1 m³	Natural gas H$_o$ (Zurich)	37.6	1.28	0.88	1.05	0.82	1.00	1.11	10.44	2.43	3.11	2.09
1 m³	Natural gas H$_u$ (Zurich)	33.8	1.15	0.79	0.94	0.73	0.90	1.00	9.39	2.18	2.79	1.88
1 kWh	Electricity	3.6	0.12	0.08	0.10	0.08	0.10	0.11	1.00	0.23	0.30	0.20
1 kg	Wood (air-dried)	15.5	0.53	0.36	0.43	0.34	0.41	0.46	4.31	1.00	1.28	0.86
1 kg	Wood chips	12.1	0.41	0.28	0.34	0.26	0.32	0.36	3.36	0.78	1.00	0.67
1 kg	Wood pellets	18.0	0.61	0.42	0.50	0.39	0.48	0.53	5.00	1.16	1.49	1.00

All calculations are based on SIA 180/4 1982 and referred to the lower calorific value H$_u$
(except fuel oil and ntural gas).

CHARACTERISTIC VALUES OF BUILDING MATERIALS
after SN EN 12524; 2000 (SIA 381.101; 2000)

Substance group or utilisation	Gross density	Thermal conductivity	Specific heat storage capacity	Water vapour diffusion resistance figure	
	ρ [kg/m³]	λ [W/(m·K)]	c_p [J/(kg·K)]	μ [–], dry	μ [–], wet
Soil					
Clay or slush or silt	1,200–1,800	1.5	1,670–2,500	50	50
Sand and gravel	1,700–2,200	2.0	910–1,180	50	50
Rock					
Cristalline rock	2,800	3.5	1,000	10,000	10,000
Sedimentary rock	2,600	2.3	1,000	250	200
Light sedimentary rock	1,500	0.85	1,000	30	20
Porous rock, e.g. lava	1,600	0.55	1,000	20	15
Basalt	2,700–3,000	3.5	1,000	10,000	10,000
Gneiss	2,400–2,700	3.5	1,000	10,000	10,000
Granite	2,500–2,700	2.8	1,000	10,000	10,000
Marble	2,800	3.5	1,000	10,000	10,000
Slate	2,000–2,800	2.2	1,000	1,000	800
Limestone, extra soft	1,600	0.85	1,000	30	20
Limestone, soft	1,800	1.1	1,000	40	25
Limestone, semi-hard	2,000	1.4	1,000	50	40
Limestone, hard	2,200	1.7	1,000	200	150
Limestone, extra-hard	2,600	2.3	1,000	250	200
Sandstone (quartzite)	2,600	2.3	1,000	40	30
Natural pumice	400	0.12	1,000	8	6
Artificial stone	1,750	1.3	1,000	50	40
Concrete*					
Average gross density	1,800	1.15	1,000	100	60
	2,000	1.35	1,000	100	60
	2,200	1.65	1,000	120	70
High gross density	2,400	2.00	1,000	130	80
Reinforced (1% steel)	2,300	2.3	1,000	130	80
Reinforced (2% steel)	2,400	2.5	1,000	130	80

* The gross density of concrete is given as dry gross density

Substance group or utilisation	Gross density	Thermal conductivity	Specific heat storage capacity	Water vapour diffusion resistance figure	
	ρ [kg/m³]	λ [W/(m·K)]	c_p [J/(kg·K)]	μ [–], dry	μ [–], wet

Masonry unplastered

Substance group or utilisation	Gross density	Thermal conductivity	Specific heat storage capacity	μ [–], dry	μ [–], wet
MB, modular brick	1,100	0.44	940	6	4
MBD, bond modular brick	1,100	0.37	940	6	4
MBLD, light brick (according to specific manufacturer's declaration)	780–850	0.11–0.12	940	6	4
	680–750	0.10–0.11	940	6	4
	620–680	0.09–0.10	940	6	4
MBLD, bond light brick (e.g. Optitherm™)	1,200	0.165	940	6	4
MBLD, bond light brick (e.g. Optitop™)	1,150	0.12	940	6	4
HTI brick high temperature insulating brick	1,200	0.47	940	6	4
MBD, face brick	1,400	0.52	940	8	6
MBD, clinker brick	1,800	1.8	940	100	
MB, full brick	1,800	0.8	940	10	8
Hearthstone	1,800	0.80	900	10	8
Sand-lime brick	1,600	0.80	900	25	10
	1,800	1.00	900	25	10
	2,000	1.10	900	25	10
Cement brick	2,000	1.10	1,000	15	10
Cement block	1,200	0.70	1,000	15	10
Breeze block	300	0.10	1,000	10	5
	400	0.13	1,000	10	5
	500	0.16	1,000	10	5
	600	0.19	1,000	10	5

Roofing tiles

Substance group or utilisation	Gross density	Thermal conductivity	Specific heat storage capacity	μ [–], dry	μ [–], wet
Clay	2,000	1.0	800	40	30
Concrete	2,100	1.5	1,000	100	60

MB: Masonry, bricks
MBL: Masonry, light bricks
D: Declared masonry

Substance group or utilisation	Gross density	Thermal conductivity	Specific heat storage capacity	Water vapour diffusion resistance figure	
	ρ [kg/m³]	λ [W/(m·K)]	c_p [J/(kg·K)]	μ [–], dry	μ [–], wet
Gypsum					
Gypsum	600	0.18	1,000	10	4
Gypsum	900	0.30	1,000	10	4
Gypsum	1,200	0.43	1,000	10	4
Gypsum	1,500	0.56	1,000	10	4
Gypsum plasterboard**	900	0.25	1,000	10	4
Plasters and mortars					
Stucco, insulating	600	0.18	1,000	10	6
Stucco	1,000	0.40	1,000	10	6
Stucco	1,300	0.57	1,000	10	6
Gypsum, sand	1,600	0.80	1,000	10	6
Lime, sand	1,600	0.80	1,000	10	6
Cement, sand	1,800	1.00	1,000	10	6
Plaster, mortar layers					
Stucco, for standard computation	1,400	0.70	900	10	6
Plaster, for standard computation	1,800	0.87	1,000	35	15
Insulating plaster, external	450	0.14	1,000	15	10
Insulating plaster, external	300	0.08	1,000	15	10
Lime mortar	1,800	0.87	1,000	35	15
Lime cement mortar	1,900	1.00	1,000	35	15
Cement mortar	2,200	1.40	1,000	35	15
Light mortar	450	0.16	1,000	20	5
	600	0.21	1,000	20	5
	900	0.32	1,000	20	5
	1,600	0.80	1,000	35	15

** The heat flux capacity includes the influence of the paper cover layer.

Substance group or utilisation	Gross density	Thermal conductivity	Specific heat storage capacity	Water vapour diffusion resistance figure	
	ρ [kg/m³]	λ [W/(m·K)]	c_p [J/(kg·K)]	μ [–], dry	μ [–], wet

Timber***

| | 500 | 0.13 | 1,600 | 50 | 20 |
| | 700 | 0.18 | 1,600 | 200 | 50 |

Timber-based materials

Plywood panel****	300	0.09	1,600	150	50
	500	0.13	1,600	200	70
	700	0.17	1,600	220	90
	1,000	0.24	1,600	250	110
Cement-bound chipboard	1,200	0.23	1,500	50	30
Chipboard	300	0.10	1,700	50	10
	600	0.14	1,700	50	15
	900	0.18	1,700	50	20
Chipboard, OSB board	650	0.13	1,700	50	30
Fibreboard, including medium density fibreboard (MDF)	250	0.07	1,700	5	2
	400	0.10	1,700	10	5
	600	0.14	1,700	20	12
	800	0.18	1,700	30	20

*** The gross density of timber and timber-based materials is the balance density at 20 °C and 65% relative humidity.
**** For solid wood panels (SWP) and laminated veneer lumber (LVL), the values for plywood can be used if the manufacturer has given no other indication.

Remarks
1. For computations, the ∞-value can be replaced by a random number, e.g. 106.
2. The figures for the water vapour diffusion resistance are given according to the "dry cup" and "wet cup procedures" defined in prEN ISO 12572:1999.

Substance group or utilisation	Gross density	Thermal conductivity	Specific heat storage capacity	Water vapour diffusion resistance figure
	ρ [kg/m³]	λ [W/(m·K)]	c_p [J/(kg·K)]	μ [–]

Insulating materials

Substance group or utilisation	Gross density	Thermal conductivity	Specific heat storage capacity	Water vapour diffusion resistance figure
Rockwool (with or without paper)	< 60	0.04	600	1–2
	60–120	0.036	600	1–2
	> 120	0.04	600	1–2
Mineral wool	200–500	0.06	600	4–10
Slag wool	40–200	0.06	600	4–10
Glass fibre	20–60	0.04	600	1–2
	> 60	0.036	600	1–2
Slag wool	30–70	0.06	600	1
Glass fibre and felts	<12	0.046	600	1
	12–18	0.044	600	1
	> 18	0.04	600	1
Rockwool	60–200	0.04	600	1
Reed	200–300	0.06	600	1
Coconut fibre	50–200	0.05	600	1
Hemp fibre	50–200	0.05	600	1
Cork, expanded	110–140	0.042	1,500	5–30
	150–200	0.046	1,500	5–30
Cork grit	100–150	0.046	1,500	1
Cork grit, natural	80–160	0.06	1,500	1
Cork grit, expanded	40–60	0.042	1,500	1
Foam glass	< 125	0.044	800	airtight
	130–150	0.048	800	airtight
Perlite, compressed with organic fibre	170–200	0.06	600	1–2
Perlite, vermiculite	50–130	0.07	600	1

Substance group or utilisation	Gross density	Thermal conductivity	Specific heat storage capacity	Water vapour diffusion resistance figure
	ρ [kg/m³]	λ [W/(m·K)]	c_p [J/(kg·K)]	μ [–]

Insulating materials

Substance group or utilisation		Gross density	Thermal conductivity	Specific heat storage capacity	Water vapour diffusion resistance figure
Polystyrene, expanded		15–18	0.042	1,400	20–40
		20–28	0.038	1,400	30–70
		> 30	0.036	1,400	40–100
Polystyrene, extruded		> 25	0.036	1,400	80–150
Polystyrene, extruded, with skin		> 30	0.034	1,400	80–300
Polyurethane (PUR)		30–80	0.03	1,400	30–100
Polyisocyanurate (PIR)		35–80	0.03	1,400	30–100
Polyethylene (PE)		30–50	0.05	1,400	400–2,000
Urea-formaldehyde (UF)		6–50	0.046	1,400	2–10
Phenol-formaldehyde (PF)		30–100	0.046	1,400	30–50
Polyvinyl chloride (PVC)		20–40	0.038	1,400	240–700
		50–100	0.044	1,400	150–300
PU foam glass gravel		200–300	0.045	1,400	30–50
PU foam clay gravel		300–400	0.055	1,400	30–50

Gases

Substance group or utilisation		Gross density	Thermal conductivity	Specific heat storage capacity	Water vapour diffusion resistance figure
Air, still		1.23	0.025	1,008	1

Air layers, including radiation

Substance group or utilisation		Gross density	Thermal conductivity	Specific heat storage capacity	Water vapour diffusion resistance figure
Air, vertical layer	5 mm	1.2	0.043	1,000	1.0
	10 mm	1.2	0.065	1,000	1.0
	20 mm	1.2	0.115	1,000	1.0
	40 mm	1.2	0.221	1,000	1.0
Air, horizontal layer heat flux from bottom to top	10 mm	1.2	0.072	1,000	1.0
	20 mm	1.2	0.137	1,000	1.0
	50 mm	1.2	0.307	1,000	1.0
Air, horizontal layer heat flux from top to bottom	10 mm	1.2	0.061	1,000	1.0
	20 mm	1.2	0.110	1,000	1.0
	50 mm	1.2	0.243	1,000	1.0

Substance group or utilisation	Gross density	Thermal conductivity	Specific heat storage capacity	Water vapour diffusion resistance figure	
	ρ [kg/m³]	λ [W/(m · K)]	c_p [J/(kg · K)]	μ [–], dry	μ [–], wet
Asphalt					
	2,100	0.70	1,000	50,000	50,000
Bitumen					
Material	1,050	0.17	1,000	50,000	50,000
Membrane/film	1,100	0.23	1,000	50,000	50,000
Floor coverings					
Synthetic material	1,700	0.25	1,400	10,000	10,000
Underlay, porous rubber or plastic	270	0.10	1,400	10,000	10,000
Felt underlay	120	0.05	1,300	20	15
Wool underlay	200	0.06	1,300	20	15
Cork underlay	< 200	0.05	1,500	20	10
Cork tile	> 400	0.065	1,500	40	20
Carpet/carpet flooring	200	0.06	1,300	5	5
Linoleum	1,200	0.17	1,400	1,000	800
Rubber	1,200	0.17	1,400	10,000	10,000
Rubber					
Natural caoutchouc	910	0.13	1,100	10,000	10,000
Neoprene (polychloroprene)	1,240	0.23	2,140	10,000	10,000
Butyl rubber, (isobutene-isoprene rubber), hard/hot melted	1,200	0.24	1,400	200,000	200,000
Foam rubber	60–80	0.06	1,500	7,000	7,000
Hard rubber (ebonite)	1,200	0.17	1,400	∞	∞
Ethylene-propylene-diene monomer (EPDM)	1,150	0.25	1,000	6,000	6,000
Polyisobutylene rubber	930	0.20	1,100	10,000	10,000
Polysulphide	1,700	0.40	1,000	10,000	10,000
Butadiene	980	0.25	1,000	100,000	100,000

Substance group or utilisation	Gross density	Thermal conductivity	Specific heat storage capacity	Water vapour diffusion resistance figure	
	ρ [kg/m³]	λ [W/(m·K)]	c_p [J/(kg·K)]	μ dry	μ wet

Tiles

Ceramic/porcelain	2,300	1.3	840		
Synthetic material	1,000	0.20	1,000	10,000	10,000

Bulk solid materials

Acrylic	1,050	0.20	1,500	10,000	10,000
Polycarbonate	1,200	0.20	1,200	5,000	5,000
Teflon (PTFE)	2,200	0.25	1,000	10,000	10,000
Polyvinyl chloride (PVC)	1,390	0.17	900	50,000	50,000
Polymethyl methacrylate (PMMA)	1,180	0.18	1,500	50,000	50,000
Polyacetal	1,410	0.30	1,400	100,000	100,000
Polyamide (nylon)	1,150	0.25	1,600	50,000	50,000
Polyamide 6.6 with 25% glass fibres	1,450	0.30	1,600	50,000	50,000
Polyethylene/high density	980	0.50	1,800	100,000	100,000
Polyethylene/low density	920	0.33	2,200	100,000	100,000
Polystyrene	1,050	0.16	1,300	100,000	100,000
Polypropylene (PP)	910	0.22	1,800	10,000	10,000
Polypropylene with 25% glass fibres	1,200	0.25	1,800	10,000	10,000
Polyurethane (PU)	1,200	0.25	1,800	6,000	6,000
Epoxy resin	1,200	0.20	1,400	10,000	10,000
Phenol resin	1,300	0.30	1,700	100,000	100,000
Polyester resin	1,400	0.19	1,200	10,000	10,000

Substance group or utilisation	Gross density	Thermal conductivity	Specific heat storage capacity	Water vapour diffusion resistance figure	
	ρ [kg/m³]	λ [W/(m·K)]	c_p [J/(kg·K)]	μ dry	μ wet

Sealing materials and insulating separators

Substance group or utilisation	Gross density	Thermal conductivity	Specific heat storage capacity	μ dry	μ wet
Silica gel (desiccant)	720	0.13	1,000	∞	∞
Silicone without extender	1,200	0.35	1,000	5,000	5,000
Silicone with extender	1,450	0.50	1,000	5,000	5,000
Silicone foam	750	0.12	1,000	10,000	10,000
Urethane/polyurethane foam (as insulating separator)	1,300	0.21	1,800	60	60
Soft polyvinylchloride (PVC-P) with 40% plasticizer	1,200	0.14	1,000	100,000	100,000
Elastomer seal foam, flexible	60–80	0.05	1,500	10,000	10,000
Polyurethane foam (PU)	70	0.05	1,500	60	60
Polyethylene foam	70	0.05	2,300	100	100

Glass

Substance group or utilisation	Gross density	Thermal conductivity	Specific heat storage capacity	μ dry	μ wet
Sodium bicarbonate glass (including float glass)	2,500	1.00	750	∞	∞

Substance group or utilisation	Gross density	Thermal conductivity	Specific heat storage capacity	Water vapour diffusion resistance figure	
	ρ [kg/m³]	λ [W/(m·K)]	c_p [J/(kg·K)]	μ dry	μ wet

Metals

Aluminium alloy	2,800	160	880	∞	∞
Bronze	8,700	65	380	∞	∞
Brass	8,400	120	380	∞	∞
Copper	8,900	380	380	∞	∞
Cast iron	7,500	50	450	∞	∞
Lead, plumbum	11,300	35	130	∞	∞
Steel	7,800	50	450	∞	∞
Stainless steel	7,900	17	460	∞	∞
Zinc	7,200	110	380	∞	∞

Water

Snow, just fallen (< 30 mm)	100	0.05	2,000		
Fresh snow, soft (3–70 mm)	200	0.12	2,000		
Snow, slightly crusted over (7–100 mm)	300	0.23	2,000		
Snow, crusted over (< 200 mm)	500	0.60	2,000		
Water, standing					

RADIATION BASED HEAT TRANSMITTANCE RHT AND TEMPERATURE TRANSMITTANCE TT

Typical constructions (materials and layers) for computing the values for RHT I, RHT II, TT I, TT II

www.pinpoint-online.ch

Construction material and layer	Material thickness	Thermal conductiv- ity	Specific heat capacity	Specific density	Heat trans- mission resistance	Heat transmis- sion coefficient
	d [mm]	λ [W/mK]	c [J/kgK]	ρ [kg/m³]	R [m²K/W]	U [W/m²K]

Single-leaf masonry

1 Masonry, plastered						
Exterior					0.04	1.83
Plaster	20	0.87	1,100	1,800	0	
Brick	150	0.44	900	1,100	0	
Plaster	10	0.6	1,100	1,800	0	
Interior					0.125	
2 Insulating bricks masonry						
Exterior					0.04	0.388
Plaster	20	0.87	1,100	1,800	0	
Insulating bricks, e.g. Optitherm™	475	0.2	900	1,100	0	
Plaster	10	0.6	1,100	1,800	0	
Interior					0.125	

Double-leaf masonry

3 Facing masonry, brick						
Exterior					0.04	0.184
Clay brick	120	0.44	900	1,100	0	
Cavity, air layer	50	0.2	1,000	1.2	0	
Rockwool	200	0.04	600	100	0	
Clay brick	150	0.44	900	1,100	0	
Interior					0.125	
4 Facing masonry, sand-lime brick						
Exterior					0.04	0.191
Sand-lime brick	120	1	900	1,800	0	
Cavity, air layer	50	0.2	1,000	1.2	0	
Rockwool	200	0.04	600	100	0	
Sand-lime brick	150	1	900	1,800	0	
Interior					0.125	

Construction material and layer	Material thickness	Thermal conductiv-ity	Specific heat capacity	Specific density	Heat trans-mission resistance	Heat transmis-sion coefficient
	d [mm]	λ [W/mK]	c [J/kgK]	ρ [kg/m³]	R [m²K/W]	U [W/m²K]

Exterior insulation

5 Exterior insulation, polystyrene						
Exterior					0.04	0.198
Plaster	20	0.87	1,100	1,800	0	
Polystyrene	180	0.04	1,400	30	0	
Clay brick	150	0.44	900	1,100	0	
Plaster	10	0.6	1,100	1,800	0	
Interior					0.125	

6 Exterior insulation, mineral wool, brick						
Exterior					0.04	0.198
Plaster	20	0.87	1,100	1,800	0	
Rockwool	180	0.04	600	100	0	
Clay brick	150	0.44	900	1,100	0	
Plaster	10	0.6	1,100	1,800	0	
Interior					0.125	

7 Exterior insulation, mineral wool, sand-lime brick						
Exterior					0.04	0.187
Plaster	20	0.87	1,100	1,800	0	
Rockwool	200	0.04	600	100	0	
Sand-lime brick	150	1	900	1,800	0	
Plaster	10	0.6	1,100	1,800	0	
Interior					0.125	

Back-ventilated facade

8 Sheet cladding, fibre cement						
Exterior					0.04	0.184
Fibre cement sheet	10	1.2	900	1,400	0	
Air layer	50	0.2	1,000	1.2	0	
Rockwool	200	0.04	600	100	0	
Clay brick	150	0.44	900	1,100	0	
Plaster	10	0.6	1,100	1,800	0	
Interior					0.125	

Construction material and layer	Material thickness	Thermal conductivity	Specific heat capacity	Specific density	Heat transmission resistance	Heat transmission coefficient
	d [mm]	λ [W/mK]	c [J/kgK]	ρ [kg/m³]	R [m²K/W]	U [W/m²K]

Panel without back-ventilation

9 Metal sheet						
Exterior					0.04	0.194
Aluminium sheet	3	220	900	2,700	0	
Rockwool	200	0.04	600	100	0	
Steel sheet	2	55	500	7,850	0	
Interior					0.125	

Wood frame construction

10 Wooden cladding, back-ventilated						
Exterior					0.04	0.191
Wooden planks	19	0.16	2,200	500	0	
Air layer	40	0.2	1,000	1.2	0	
Rockwool	200	0.04	600	100	0	
Wooden planks	24	0.16	2,200	500	0	
Interior					0.125	

Interior insulation

11 Fair-face concrete facade						
Exterior					0.04	0.185
Fair-face concrete	200	1.8	1,100	2,400	0	
Rockwool	200	0.04	600	100	0	
Wooden panelling	22	0.16	2,200	500	0	
Interior					0.125	

12 Quarry stone facade						
Exterior					0.04	0.186
Quarry stone	600	1	900	1,600	0	
Rockwool	180	0.04	600	100	0	
Plasterboard	25	0.21	800	900	0	
Interior					0.125	

Construction material and layer	Material thickness	Thermal conductivity	Specific heat capacity	Specific density	Heat transmission resistance	Heat transmission coefficient
	d [mm]	λ [W/mK]	c [J/kgK]	ρ [kg/m³]	R [m²K/W]	U [W/m²K]

Interior insulation

13 Quarry stone, plastered facade						
Exterior					0.04	0.188
Plaster	20	0.87	1,100	1,800	0	
Quarry stone masonry	600	1	900	1,600	0	
Rockwool	180	0.04	600	100	0	
Plaster	20	0.6	1,100	1,800	0	
Interior					0.125	

Flat roof

14 Flat roof, gravelled						
Exterior					0.04	0.155
Gravel	100	0.7	800	1,800	0	
Polyurethane foam	180	0.03	1,400	80	0	
Concrete	240	1.8	1,100	2,400	0	
Interior					0.125	

Pitched roof

15 Tile cladding						
Exterior					0.04	0.192
Tile	50	0.5	900	1,400	0	
Air layer	100	0.2	1,000	1.2	0	
Rockwool	200	0.04	600	100	0	
Wooden cladding	19	0.16	2,200	500	0	
Interior					0.125	

16 Tile cladding, PAVATHERM						
Exterior					0.04	0.168
Tile	50	0.5	900	1,400	0	
Air layer	100	0.2	1,000	1.2	0	
PAVATHERM	30	0.04	600	100	0	
Rockwool	200	0.04	600	100	0	
Wooden cladding	19	0.16	2,200	500	0	
Interior					0.125	

Construction material and layer	Material thickness	Thermal conductivity	Specific heat capacity	Specific density	Heat transmission resistance	Heat transmission coefficient
	d [mm]	λ [W/mK]	c [J/kgK]	ρ [kg/m³]	R [m²K/W]	U [W/m²K]

Interior building components, floor slabs

17 Reinforced concrete						
Exterior					0.167	2.140
Reinforced concrete	240	1.8	1,100	2,400	0	
Interior					0.167	
18 Reinforced concrete, with carpet						
Exterior					0.167	1.620
Carpet	12	0.08	1,000	300	0	
Reinforced concrete	240	1.8	1,100	2,400	0	
Interior					0.167	
19 Reinforced concrete, screed						
Exterior					0.167	0.764
Carpet	12	0.08	1,000	300	0	
Screed	80	0.87	1,100	1,800	0	
Impact noise insulation	30	0.05	1,500	150	0	
Concrete	240	1.8	1,100	2,400	0	
Interior					0.167	

Partition walls

20 Clay brick wall						
Exterior					0.125	1.692
Clay brick	150	0.44	900	1,100	0	
Interior					0.125	
21 Sand-lime brick wall						
Exterior					0.125	2.500
Sand-lime brick	150	1	900	1,800	0	
Interior					0.125	
22 Plasterboard wall						
Exterior					0.125	0.348
Plasterboard	25	0.4	800	1,000	0	
Rockwool	100	0.04	600	100	0	
Plasterboard	25	0.4	800	1,000	0	
Interior					0.125	

RADIATION BASED HEAT AND TEMPERATURE TRANSMITTANCE, RHT AND TT

	Construction material and layer	U-value	TT I iso	TT II adia	RHT I iso	RHT II adia	Temp. ampl.	Heat flux ampl.	Temp. phase shift h	Heat flux phase shift h
	Exterior building components									
1	Masonry, plastered	1.83	1.2730	0.2101	0.0509	0.0084	4.76	19.64	8.06	19.64
2	Insulating brick masonry	0.388	0.0072	0.0014	0.0003	0.0001	713.83	3,471.19	3.23	23.89
3	Facing brick masonry, double-leaf	0.184	0.0304	0.0056	0.0012	0.0002	177.47	821.09	16.81	13.85
4	Facing sand-lime brick masonry, double-leaf	0.191	0.0296	0.0033	0.0012	0.0001	305.87	843.18	16.23	13.38
5	Exterior insulation, polystyrene, BS	0.198	0.0599	0.0200	0.0024	0.0008	50.04	417.05	14.23	6.99
6	Exterior insulation, rockwool, brick	0.198	0.0572	0.0187	0.0023	0.0007	53.46	436.84	14.86	7.46
7	Exterior insulation, rockwool, sand-lime brick	0.187	0.0444	0.0145	0.0018	0.0006	69.20	562.99	15.05	7.63
8	Sheet cladding, rockwool, sand-lime brick	0.184	0.0472	0.0404	0.0019	0.0016	24.74	529.72	15.00	9.43
9	Metal panel	0.194	0.1727	0.2077	0.0069	0.0083	4.81	144.80	7.80	3.18
10	Wood frame construction	0.191	0.1389	0.0677	0.0056	0.0027	14.76	179.99	10.21	5.43
11	Fair-face concrete, interior insulation	0.185	0.0457	0.0037	0.0018	0.0001	268.13	546.72	12.73	6.23
12	Quarry stone, interior insulation	0.186	0.0036	0.0005	0.0001	0.00002	2,158.14	6,966.14	22.84	20.68
13	Quarry stone, interior insulation, plastered	0.188	0.0030	0.0004	0.0001	0.00003	2,695.18	8,469.23	0.07	21.87
14	Flat roof	0.155	0.0086	0.0012	0.0003	0.00005	865.48	2,904.36	20.69	17.53
15	Pitched roof	0.192	0.1292	0.0294	0.0052	0.00120	33.96	193.50	10.46	5.94
16	Pitched roof, wood fibre board	0.168	0.1050	0.0239	0.0042	0.00100	41.86	238.12	11.28	6.17
	Interior building components									
17	Reinforced concrete	2.14	0.4243	0.0877	0.0709	0.01470	11.40	14.11	9.00	6.67
18	Reinforced concrete, carpet	1.62	0.2457	0.0869	0.0410	0.01450	11.51	24.37	9.11	7.17
19	Reinforced concrete, screed	0.764	0.0293	0.0107	0.0049	0.00180	93.66	204.54	15.31	14.34
20	Partition wall, brick	1.692	1.1671	0.3341	0.1459	0.04180	2.99	6.85	6.48	4.58
21	Partition wall, sand-lime brick	2.500	1.4709	0.2950	0.1839	0.03690	3.39	5.44	6.29	4.87
22	Partition wall, plasterboard	0.348	0.3276	0.2157	0.0409	0.02700	4.64	24.42	6.76	2.50

Phase differences for massive constructions can be shifted by +24 h.

U-value computations of back-ventilated constructions
see page 37

MEAN MONTHLY AND ANNUAL TEMPERATURES θ_{am} [°C]
LONG-THERM MEAN VALUES 1961–1970
SIA 381/3

Climate regions of Switzerland
1: Eatern Jura
2: Western Jura
3: Northeastern Plateau
4: Central Plateau
5: Western Plateau
6: Eastern Alps, north side
7: Central Alps, north side
8: Western Alps, north side
9: North and central Grisons
10: Valais
11: Engadine
12: Alps, south side

Position of weather station
F: Lowlands, shallow valley
A: Higher positions, hills
T: Sloped valley
M: Hollow position, narrow valley
U: Lakeside
■: Dense urban context
S, E, W, N: south, east, west, north side
P: Pass, col
G: Summit, peak, ridge

Station	Climate region	Position	Altitude above sea level
Airolo	12	T	1,167
Altdorf	7	F	449
Arosa	9	E	1,865
Bad Ragaz	9	F	518
Basel-Binningen	1	A	316
Beatenberg	8	S	1,180
Bern	4	A ■	572
Bever	11	F	1,712
Beznau	3	F	330
Biel	4	F	434
Château-d'Oex	8	HS	994
La Chaux-de-Fonds	2	H ■	990
Chippis	10	F	552
Chur	9	F	582
Comprovasco	12	HT	544
Davos	9	A	1,561
Delémont	2	F	416
Disentis	9	S	1,173
Einsiedeln	7	F	914
Engelberg	7	T	1,018
Fey-Nendaz	10	N	780
Fribourg	5	A	677
Geneva	5	A ■	405
Glarus	6	T	480
Göschenen	7	T	1,109
Heiden	6	T	809
Interlaken	8	S	568
Jungfraujoch	8	S	3,576
Kreuzlingen	3	S	446
Langenbruck	2	F ■	740
Langnau i. E.	7	F	692

Month												Year	Sep–May
Jan	Feb	Mar	Apr	May	Jun	Jul	Aug	Sep	Oct	Nov	Dec		
-2.9	-1.4	1.2	5.1	9.2	13.3	15.4	14.4	11.8	7.5	1.7	-2.2	6.14	3.37
0.2	1.9	4.4	9.2	12.8	16.3	17.7	16.8	14.6	10.2	5.6	0.2	9.20	6.59
-5.4	-5.5	-3.4	0.6	4.3	8.4	10.3	9.7	8.1	4.9	-0.8	-5.2	2.20	-0.25
-0.9	1.3	4.2	9.2	12.7	16.3	17.7	16.7	14.6	10.1	5.0	-1.4	8.83	6.11
0.0	2.1	4.8	9.5	13.0	16.7	18.3	17.3	15.0	10.4	5.0	0.3	9.42	6.72
-1.5	-0.4	1.6	5.7	9.3	12.8	14.8	14.0	12.4	8.8	3.4	-1.0	6.69	4.28
-1.3	1.0	3.8	8.6	12.4	16.2	18.0	16.9	14.5	9.8	4.1	-0.8	8.64	5.81
-9.7	-7.7	-4.4	0.7	5.5	9.5	11.0	10.2	7.6	3.2	-2.9	-9.4	1.17	-1.88
-0.5	1.4	4.0	8.8	12.4	16.4	18.0	16.8	14.5	10.1	4.8	0.2	8.94	6.20
-1.2	0.9	3.6	8.5	12.3	16.3	18.1	16.9	14.4	9.5	4.2	-0.4	8.63	5.87
-3.4	-1.7	1.0	5.7	9.6	13.2	15.0	13.9	11.8	7.5	2.0	-3.1	6.00	3.29
-1.3	0.0	2.0	6.5	10.2	13.9	15.7	14.7	12.8	9.0	3.6	-1.0	7.23	4.69
-1.2	1.6	5.1	10.2	14.2	17.8	19.2	17.7	15.1	10.1	4.4	-1.1	9.46	6.51
-0.7	1.3	4.4	9.2	12.8	16.5	18.0	16.9	14.9	10.6	5.0	-1.3	9.00	6.27
0.4	2.1	5.3	9.4	12.8	16.4	18.2	17.2	14.5	10.3	4.9	1.3	9.44	6.81
-6.2	-5.4	-2.6	2.4	6.7	10.6	12.3	11.4	9.3	5.2	-0.6	-6.0	3.12	0.31
-1.0	1.1	3.7	8.2	11.9	15.7	17.2	16.4	14.1	9.9	4.3	-0.6	8.45	5.76
-1.9	-1.2	1.3	5.7	9.5	13.4	15.2	14.3	12.5	8.7	3.1	-1.8	6.61	4.01
-2.9	-1.3	0.9	5.6	9.6	13.5	15.2	14.2	12.1	7.8	2.9	-2.7	6.28	3.59
-3.2	-1.7	0.4	5.2	9.2	12.8	14.3	13.3	11.4	7.4	2.2	-3.4	5.69	3.07
-1.2	0.7	3.5	8.1	12.1	15.7	17.6	16.2	13.9	9.6	4.0	-0.8	8.32	5.56
-1.5	0.6	3.2	7.9	11.7	15.5	17.3	16.1	13.8	9.3	3.6	-1.1	8.08	5.30
0.9	2.8	5.4	10.0	13.9	17.7	19.9	18.9	16.1	11.4	6.0	1.6	10.42	7.59
-2.0	0.2	2.9	8.3	12.0	15.6	17.0	16.0	13.9	9.5	4.1	-1.9	8.01	5.23
-2.6	-1.8	0.4	4.5	8.4	12.2	13.9	13.1	11.5	7.6	2.3	-2.4	5.65	3.13
-2.0	-0.6	1.7	6.7	10.2	13.9	15.3	14.5	12.7	8.5	3.5	-2.2	6.88	4.29
-1.4	0.4	3.2	8.3	12.2	15.7	17.4	16.1	13.8	9.1	3.8	-0.9	8.20	5.43
-14.1	-15.0	-13.2	-10.9	-7.0	-3.0	-1.2	-1.5	-2.2	-4.6	-10.2	-14.0	-6.04	-10.12
-0.9	0.8	3.6	8.7	12.2	16.0	17.7	16.7	14.3	9.7	4.4	-0.5	6.59	5.82
-2.0	-2.0	2.1	7.1	10.9	14.7	16.4	15.4	13.3	8.8	3.1	-1.8	7.35	4.61
-1.9	0.3	2.9	7.6	11.5	15.3	16.9	15.7	13.5	9.2	3.6	-1.4	7.81	5.06

Station	Climate region	Position	Altitude above sea level
Lausanne	5	F	589
Leysin	8	F	1,350
Locarno-Monti	12	S	379
Lugano	12	A	275
Lucerne	4	S	498
Marsens	5	A	721
Meiringen	8	F	605
Montana	10	F	1,509
Montreux	5	G	376
Mt-Soleil	2	S	1,183
Neuchâtel	5	A	487
Oeschberg	4	F	483
Otten	4	F	412
Rigi-Kulm	7	G	1,775
Robbia	12	T	1,078
Säntis	6	G	2,500
Schaffhausen	3	E	435
Scuol	11	S	1,253
Sion	10	A	549
Gr. St. Bernhard	10	HP	2,472
St. Gallen	3	T	664
St. Gotthard	12	P	2,095
St. Moritz	11	A	1,833
Weissfluhjoch	9	G	2,667
Zermatt	10	T	1,610
Zurich Bot. Garten	3	U ■	411
Zurich-SMA	3	S	556

Month												Year	Sep–May
Jan	Feb	Mar	Apr	May	Jun	Jul	Aug	Sep	Oct	Nov	Dec		
0.0	1.9	4.6	9.3	13.0	16.7	18.8	17.6	15.1	10.8	5.1	0.3	9.47	6.70
-1.6	-1.3	0.7	4.8	8.6	12.3	14.2	13.2	11.5	8.0	2.8	-1.4	6.02	3.59
2.3	4.1	7.6	11.7	15.3	18.8	20.9	19.9	17.1	12.5	6.9	3.2	11.74	8.99
1.9	3.9	7.3	11.5	15.4	19.1	21.4	20.4	17.6	13.0	7.3	2.8	11.83	8.98
-1.1	1.1	3.9	8.8	12.4	16.1	17.9	16.8	14.5	9.7	4.3	-0.6	8.70	5.92
-2.1	0.3	3.1	8.1	11.3	15.2	17.0	15.8	13.2	9.1	3.6	-0.8	7.84	5.09
-1.5	0.8	3.6	8.9	12.3	15.5	16.9	16.1	14.1	9.8	4.2	-1.6	8.29	5.64
-2.4	-1.8	0.6	4.7	8.7	12.5	14.3	13.3	11.7	7.9	2.1	-2.0	5.85	3.32
0.8	2.5	5.1	9.7	13.6	17.3	19.5	18.3	15.7	11.3	6.0	1.3	10.14	7.36
-2.4	-1.8	0.2	4.6	8.1	11.8	13.5	12.9	11.4	7.9	2.0	-2.3	5.52	3.09
-0.4	1.5	4.4	9.2	13.0	16.9	18.8	17.7	15.3	10.5	4.9	0.3	9.38	6.54
-2.0	0.2	3.1	8.1	11.8	15.7	17.3	16.4	13.9	9.1	3.6	-1.1	8.05	5.21
-0.7	1.2	3.9	8.7	12.4	16.3	17.9	16.6	14.5	10.0	4.5	-0.2	8.80	6.04
-4.7	-5.1	-2.8	1.1	4.1	8.5	9.8	9.6	8.3	4.6	-0.2	-3.6	2.50	0.21
-2.5	-1.1	1.8	6.4	10.1	13.7	15.3	14.4	11.9	7.7	2.7	-1.6	6.60	3.95
-6.8	-9.2	-7.7	-4.2	-0.8	3.2	5.0	4.7	3.9	1.4	-4.4	-8.4	-2.06	-4.21
-1.4	0.8	3.7	9.0	12.5	16.3	17.8	16.6	14.2	9.5	4.0	-1.0	8.53	5.71
-6.0	-3.8	-0.1	5.2	9.6	13.3	14.8	13.6	10.9	5.7	-0.1	-5.9	4.82	1.75
-0.6	2.1	5.5	10.4	14.3	18.0	19.5	18.0	15.7	10.8	4.9	-0.4	9.90	6.98
-6.0	-9.1	-7.0	-3.8	0.3	4.4	7.4	6.9	4.9	1.8	-4.0	-8.0	-1.14	-3.63
-1.8	0.1	2.6	7.6	11.2	14.9	16.6	15.5	13.5	9.0	3.9	-1.6	7.66	4.96
-7.6	-7.6	-5.5	-1.7	1.8	5.8	8.5	7.7	6.2	2.9	-3.1	-7.1	0.06	-2.40
-7.3	-6.3	-3.7	0.9	5.3	9.2	11.0	10.2	8.1	4.1	-1.5	-6.9	1.96	-0.80
-9.5	10.1	-6.5	-5.0	-1.3	2.7	4.9	4.7	3.8	0.9	-5.0	-9.2	-2.60	-4.86
-5.0	-4.2	-1.6	2.6	6.6	10.1	11.8	10.7	9.0	5.3	-0.4	-4.7	3.40	0.88
0.1	2.1	4.8	9.7	13.6	17.6	19.3	17.9	15.6	11.0	5.4	0.6	9.85	7.01
-1.1	0.9	3.7	8.6	12.2	15.8	17.5	16.4	14.3	9.8	4.2	-0.9	8.49	5.76

MEAN MONTHLY GLOBAL HORIZONTAL IRRADIATION I, SUMMED (MJ/m²)

SIA Documentation 64, www.meteoschweiz.ch

Weather station	Alt.	Jan	Feb	Mar	Apr	May	Jun	Jul	Aug	Sep	Oct	Nov	Dec
Plateau													
Altdorf UR	449	144	222	382	491	604	636	636	556	432	294	144	103
Bad Ragaz	505	153	225	362	469	589	632	640	578	436	310	151	104
Basel Binningen BL	316	129	189	330	441	574	642	648	569	387	243	118	87
Bern-Liebefeld BE	570	126	198	338	448	577	659	664	595	402	251	120	85
Birmensdorf ZH	550	100	162	298	398	532	560	601	502	390	219	114	82
Chabies FR	565	110	184	331	463	574	661	694	562	401	242	116	85
Changins s. Nyon VD	435	127	194	342	479	579	656	691	601	427	256	126	89
Chur GR	530	165	228	378	484	587	643	652	586	435	315	156	112
Fribourg FR	634	116	177	308	450	558	643	667	571	406	252	134	93
Geneva Airport GE	416	103	178	286	487	574	550	680	578	456	232	129	101
Hallau SH	435	96	168	302	440	572	647	646	549	391	218	102	71
Huttwil BE	638	117	173	311	409	552	608	616	552	401	240	121	91
Kreuzlingen TG	445	105	174	336	468	588	653	663	586	396	232	109	74
Lausanne VD	605	120	156	259	465	563	558	632	505	423	229	124	89
Lucerne LU	498	106	175	332	443	553	597	613	529	376	225	112	77
Neuchâtel NE	487	106	182	340	465	592	686	683	606	396	225	106	74
Nidau BE	430	79	148	276	407	499	527	535	477	361	179	93	63
Oeschberg BE	483	102	173	306	431	555	637	643	555	390	228	106	74
Otten SO	412	89	151	289	415	542	591	614	526	374	205	101	69
Schaffhausen SH	437	103	170	330	449	572	642	635	555	388	221	104	73
St. Gallen SG	670	108	175	312	430	559	612	624	562	392	232	114	76
Stein AR	780	120	179	304	412	535	564	587	498	386	251	124	85
Tänikon TG	536	96	162	303	412	549	577	581	529	386	210	111	74
Winterthur ZH	495	95	175	311	426	560	592	613	542	402	223	111	72
Zurich-Kloten ZH	436	91	163	296	408	549	594	654	495	375	221	102	67
Zurich (SMA) ZH	569	114	187	336	448	584	654	660	582	390	234	113	78
Jura													
La Chaux-de-Fonds NE	1,060	144	216	364	480	576	598	610	547	398	278	149	111
Mont-Soleil BE	1,180	140	210	363	480	562	569	584	516	391	279	145	111

Weather station	Alt.	Jan	Feb	Mar	Apr	May	Jun	Jul	Aug	Sep	Oct	Nov	Dec
Rhone valley													
Chippis VS	529	133	211	343	494	577	597	634	530	403	280	146	102
Martigny VS	457	128	207	330	487	571	593	625	517	382	274	142	98
Monthey VS	405	116	179	306	473	544	555	570	562	367	244	138	98
Montreux-Clarens VD	405	129	205	358	481	590	676	691	595	411	276	135	101
Sion VS	542	122	204	333	488	555	581	593	519	400	257	152	103
Turtmann VS	622	82	165	351	494	559	583	607	543	387	211	96	77
Vernayaz VS	453	104	196	328	494	568	594	637	564	413	255	142	79
Alps													
Adelboden BE	1,355	165	249	420	548	613	581	612	531	445	314	184	143
Airolo TI	1,139	109	233	415	575	628	639	657	555	433	272	137	98
Arosa TI	1,847	170	254	433	552	615	590	602	529	431	312	184	145
Bever GR	1,712	166	259	442	263	628	613	623	555	431	304	176	135
Bivio GR	1,770	169	255	442	569	647	633	636	553	467	320	186	148
Chateau-d'Oex VD	980	166	254	432	559	637	638	656	571	446	315	180	141
Davos GR	1,588	172	247	425	546	619	605	621	530	436	315	182	143
Disentis GR	1,185	165	252	424	548	609	600	618	539	446	312	178	142
Engelberg OW	1,015	171	251	416	539	604	581	581	513	432	308	190	145
Heiligenschwendi BE	1,126	155	240	406	535	603	574	614	518	420	308	165	126
Leysin VD	1,320	130	192	322	475	547	564	576	471	352	245	140	103
Montana VS	1,500	154	229	387	530	603	617	632	543	414	288	168	126
Mürren BE	1,638	168	253	419	538	605	578	598	542	451	311	188	147
Beckingen VS	1,325	149	225	383	532	587	609	641	433	429	293	166	128
Rigi Kaltbad LU	1,453	151	239	394	525	596	546	575	505	410	289	166	136
San Bernadino GR	1,628	166	256	423	563	607	600	625	539	444	311	189	150
Scuol GR	1,250	171	255	442	569	636	630	631	554	446	306	183	142
St. Moritz GR	1,625	157	255	438	563	634	604	617	542	443	312	171	134
Zermatt VS	1,638	170	245	419	547	636	656	690	593	458	316	174	135

Weather station	Alt.	Jan	Feb	Mar	Apr	May	Jun	Jul	Aug	Sep	Oct	Nov	Dec
Summits													
Gütsch, above Andermatt UR	2,284	203	292	483	610	666	611	611	518	434	340	216	174
Jungfraujoch VS	3,580	200	285	489	610	660	597	577	491	422	341	212	167
Säntis AI/AR/SG	2,500	192	277	474	593	656	560	506	439	388	329	203	158
Weissfluhjoch GR	2,672	200	286	486	609	672	611	573	483	423	341	212	174
Ticino													
Locarno-Monti TI	366	177	244	400	515	614	658	715	594	427	300	157	145
Lugano TI	276	166	235	381	486	589	665	702	588	417	279	160	134
Monte Bre TI	905	163	216	370	464	556	638	679	532	412	296	167	149

GREY ENERGY OF BUILDING MATERIALS

Material	Density	Primary energy content	
	[kg/m³]	[MJ/kg]	[GJ/m³]
Masonry, bricks, tiles			
Brick	1,500	3.1	4.59
Modular brick	1,100	3.1	3.37
Clinker brick	2,000	3.12	6.23
Tile	1,900	2.7	5.13
Sand-lime brick	1,800	0.88	1.58
Cement brick	1,200	1.87	2.25
Aerated concrete block	600	1.98	1.19
Cement aggregates			
Sand, gravel	2,600	0.015	0.04
Expanded clay	330	3.42	1.13
Limestone, broken	2,700	0.83	2.24
Limestone, powdered	700	0.65	0.45
Natural pumice	850	0.017	0.014
Natural stone, broken	2,700	0.10	0.27
Concrete, mortar			
Concrete PC 350	2,400	0.9	2.16
Expanded clay-lightweight concrete	1,600	2.0	3.2
EPS-lightweight concrete	800	3.9	3.12
Prefabricated concrete elements, pipes	2,200	1.4	3.08
Transit mix concrete	2,300	0.8	1.84
Reinforced concrete	2,400	2.0	4.8
Cellular concrete, sheathed	600	5.8	3.48
Prefabricated reinforced concrete elements, pipes	2,200	2.9	6.38
Wood, wood-based material			
Building timber	400	19.4	7.76
Laminated wood, composite lumber	600	16.3	9.78
Wood fibreboard	700	15.8	11.1

Material	Density	Primary energy content	
	[kg/m³]	[MJ/kg]	[GJ/m³]
Non-ferrous metal			
Aluminium	2,700	165	446
Aluminium, 20% recycled	2,700	140	378
Aluminium, 100% recycled	2,700	16	43.2
Aluminium foil (10–100 μm thick)	2,700	171	462
Copper	8,900	46.8	417
Iron, ferrous material			
Cast iron	7,800	13	101
Raw steel	7,850	21	165
Steel	7,850	24	188
Steel, recycled	7,850	14.3	112
Steel, stainless	7,900	31.9	252
Profile steel	7,850	25.9	203
Concrete reinforcing steel	7,850	30.1	236
Steel sheet	7,850	32.3	254
Pre-stressing steel	7,900	34	269
Tin plate	7,850	33	260
Tin plate, 100% recycled	7,850	20	157
Glass and glass materials			
Sheet glass	2,500	8.9	22.3
Glass with 56.2% recycled glass	2,500	7	17.5
Glass, 100% recycled	2,500	5.5	13.8
Glass wool 20	20	18	0.36
Foam glass	130	11.4	1.48
Synthetic materials			
Polyethylene PE, soft	920	47	43.2
Polyethylene PE, hard	950	47	44.7
Polyvinylchloride PVC	1,400	42.5	59.5

Material	Density	Primary energy content	
	[kg/m³]	[MJ/kg]	[GJ/m³]
Insulation materials			
Polystyrene PS, expanded	20	123	2.46
Polystyrene PS, expanded, hard	60	123	7.37
Polystyrene PS, extruded	50	123	6.14
Polyurethane PUR, rigid foam	80	105	8.4
Rockwool 60	60	18	1.08
Rockwool 300	300	18	5.4
Cork 150	3.4	0.51	
Perlite	140	60.5	8.46
Various materials			
Bitumen, hot mix	1,400	0.72	1.01
Bitumen, cold mix	1,400	0.37	0.51
Plasterboard	900	3.21	2.89
Stoneware pipe	1,900	5.59	10.6

Sources:
N. Kohler: Analyse énergetique de la Construction; EPF Lausanne 1986
J. Gneiss et al.: Energieautarkes Büro und Lagergebäude; IBB Muttenz 1988
Umweltbundesamt (ed.): Ökologisches Bauen; Bauverlag 1982
P. Hofstetter: Die ökologische Rückzahldauer...; ETH Zurich 1991
K. Habersatter: Ökobilanz von Packstoffen; BUWAL Nr. 132, Bern 1991
W. Scholz: Baustoffkenntnis; Werner-Verlag, Düsseldorf 1980

RELATIONSHIP OF SIA TO EN STANDARDS

SIA no.	Prefix	EN no.	WI no.	Year
180.051	EN ISO	7345	00089031	1996
180.052	EN ISO	9251	00089042	1996
180.053	EN ISO	9288	00089033	1996
180.054	EN ISO	9346	00089032	2007
180.071	EN ISO	6946	00089013	2007
180.071/A1	EN ISO	6946/A1	00089088	2003
180.072	EN ISO	13788	00089046	2002
180.073	EN ISO	13786	00089049	2007
180.074	EN ISO	13793	00089017	2001
180.075	EN ISO	10211	00089014	2007
180.076	EN ISO	10211-2	00089076	2001
180.077	EN ISO	14683	00089015	2007
180.078	EN	13363-1	00089019	2003
180.079	EN	13363-2	00089078	2005
180.081	EN ISO	10077-1rev	00089096	2006
180.081	EN ISO	10077-1	00089018	2000
180.082	EN ISO	10077-2	00089072	2003
180.083	EN	13947	00089101	2006
181.021	EN ISO	717-1	00126011	1997
181.021/A1	EN ISO	717-1/A1	00126071	2006
181.022	EN ISO	717-2	00126012	1997
181.022/A1	EN ISO	717-2/A1	00126081	2006

Title
Thermal insulation – Physical quantities and definitions (ISO 7345:1987)
Thermal insulation – Heat transfer – Conditions and properties of materials – Vocabulary (ISO 9251:1987)
Thermal insulation – Heat transfer by radiation – Physical quantities and definitions (ISO 9288:1989)
Hygrothermal performance of buildings and building materials – Physical quantities for mass transfer – Vocabulary (ISO 9346:2007)
Building components and building elements – Thermal resistance and thermal transmittance – Calculation method (ISO 6946:2007)
Building components and building elements – Thermal resistance and thermal transmittance – Calculation method (ISO 6946:1996/AMD1:2003)
Machine tools – Safety – Multi-spindle automatic turning machines (ISO 13788:2001)
Thermal performance of building components – Dynamic thermal characteristics – Calculation methods (ISO 13786:2007)
Thermal performance of buildings – Thermal design of foundations to avoid frost heave (ISO 13793:2001)
Thermal bridges in building construction – Heat flows and surface temperatures – Detailed calculations (ISO 10211:2007)
Thermal bridges in building construction – Heat flows and surface temperatures – Part 2: Linear thermal bridges (ISO 10211-2:2001)
Thermal bridges in building construction – Linear thermal transmittance – Simplified methods and default values (ISO 14683:2007)
Solar protection devices combined with glazing – Calculation of solar and light transmittance – Part 1 : Simplified method
Solar protection devices combined with glazing – Calculation of total solar energy transmittance and light transmittance – Part 2: Detailed calculation method
Thermal performance of windows, doors and shutters – Calculation of thermal transmittance – Part 1: General (ISO 10077-1:2006)
Thermal performance of windows, doors and shutters – Calculation of thermal transmittance – Part 1: Simplified method (ISO 10077-1:2000)
Thermal performance of windows, doors and shutters – Calculation of thermal transmittance – Part 2: Numerical method for frames (ISO 10077-2:2003)
Thermal performance of curtain walling – Calculation of thermal transmittance
Acoustics – Rating of sound insulation in buildings and of building elements – Part 1: Airborne sound insulation (ISO 717-1:1996)
Acoustics – Rating of sound insulation in buildings and of building elements – Part 1: Airborne sound insulation – Amendment 1: Rounding rules related to single number ratings and single number quantities (ISO 717-1:1996/AMD1:2006)
Acoustics – Rating of sound insulation in buildings and of building elements – Part 2: Impact sound insulation (ISO 717-2:1996)
Acoustics – Rating of sound insulation in buildings and of building elements – Part 2: Impact sound insulation (ISO 717-2:1996/AMD1:2006)

SIA no.	Prefix	EN no.	WI no.	Year
181.087	EN ISO	11654	00126027	1997
181.301	EN	12354-1	00126029	2000
181.302	EN	12354-2	00126030	2000
181.303	EN	12354-3	00126031	2000
181.304	EN	12354-4	00126032	2000
181.306	EN	12354-6	00126034	2003
181.501	EN ISO	18233	00126053	2006
329.001	EN	12152	00033203	2002
329.003	EN	12154	00033205	2004
329.005	EN	12179	00033210	2000
329.007	EN	13051	00033208	2001
329.008	EN	13116	00033209	2001
329.010	EN	13830	00033238	2003
329.011	EN	14019	00033218	2004
329.xxx	prEN	13119	00033325	2007
331.100	EN	14351-1	00033279	2006
331.101	prEN	12488	00129018	2003
331.102	prEN ISO	14439	00129017	2007
331.103	prEN	13474-1	00129031	1999
331.104	prEN	13474-2	00129094	2000
331.151	EN	410	00129030	1998
331.152	EN	673	00129014	1998
331.152/A1	EN	673/A1	00129096	2000
331.152/A2	EN	673/A2	00129120	2002
331.156	EN	12898	00129045	2001
331.158	EN ISO	14438	00129016	2002
331.158	EN ISO	14438	00129016	2002
331.161	EN	12758	00129032	2002
331.301	EN	12207	00033021	2000
331.302	EN	12208	00033023	2000
331.303	EN	12210	00033025	2000

Title
Acoustics – Sound absorbers for use in buildings – Rating of sound absorption (ISO 11654:1997)
Building acoustics – Estimation of acoustic performance in buildings from the performance of elements – Part 1: Airborne sound insulation between rooms
Building acoustics – Estimation of acoustic performance in buildings from the performance of elements – Part 2: Impact sound insulation between rooms
Building acoustics – Estimation of acoustic performance in buildings from the performance of elements – Part 3: Airborne sound insultation against outdoor sound
Building acoustics – Estimation of acoustic performance in buildings from the performance of elements – Part 4: Transmission of indoor sound to the outside
Building acoustics – Estimation of acoustic performance of buildings from the performance of elements – Part 6: Sound absorption in enclosed spaces
Acoustics – Application of new measurement methods in building and room acoustics (ISO 18233:2006)
Curtain walling – Air permeability – Performance requirements and classification
Curtain walling – Watertightness – Performance requirements and classification
Curtain walling – Resistance to wind load – Test method
Curtain walling – Watertightness – Site test
Curtain walling – Resistance to wind load – Performance requirements
Curtain walling – Product standard
Curtain walling – Impact resistance – Performance requirements
Curtain walling – Terminology
Windows and doors – Product standard, performance characteristics – Part 1: Windows and external pedestrian doorsets without resistance to fire and/or smoke leakage characteristics
Glass in building – Glazing requirements – Assembly rules
Glass in building – Assembly rules – Glazing wedges
Glass in building – Design of glass panes – Part 1: General basis of design
Glass in building – Design of glass panes – Part 2: Design for uniformly distributed loads
Glass in building – Determination of luminous and solar characteristics of glazing
Glass in building – Determination of thermal transmittance (U value) – Calculation method
Glass in building – Determination of thermal transmittance (U value) – Calculation method
Glass in building – Determination of thermal transmittance (U value) – Calculation method
Glass in building – Determination of the emissivity
Glass in building – Determination of energy balance value – Calculation method
Glass in building – Determination of energy balance value – Calculation method (ISO 14438:2002)
Glass in building – Glazing and airborne sound insulation – Product descriptions and determination of properties
Windows and doors – Air permeability – Classification
Windows and doors – Watertightness – Classification
Windows and doors – Resistance to wind load – Classification

SIA no.	Prefix	EN no.	WI no.	Year
331.303/AC	EN	12210/AC	00033C03	2003
331.307	EN	1191	00033053	2000
331.308	EN	12400	00033176	2002
342.010	EN	12216	00033142	2002
342.011	EN	13125	00033100	2001
342.016	EN	13561	00033143	2004
342.017	EN	13659	00033234	2004
342.018	EN	14759	00033099	2005
342.019	EN	14501	00033175	2005
380.101	EN	832	00089020	2000
380.101/AC	EN	832/AC	00089C03	2002
380.102	EN ISO	13789	00089043	2007
380.103	EN ISO	13370	00089016	2007
380.104	EN ISO	13790	00089063	2008
380.301	EN ISO	13787	00089036	2003
380.302	EN ISO	8497	00089053	1997
380.303	EN ISO	12241	00089007	2008
380.304	EN	14114	00089083	2002
381.101	EN	12524	00089012	2000
381.201	EN ISO	15927-1	00089027	2006
381.204	EN ISO	15927-4	00089069	2005
381.205	EN ISO	15927-5	00089068	2006
382.101	CR	1752	00156056	1999
382.102	EN	12599/AC	00156C01	2002
382.102	EN	12599	00156059	2000
382.103	EN	12792	00156076	2003
382.201	EN	13465	00156033	2004
382.202	EN	14134	00156032	2004
382.203	CEN/TR	14788	00156064	2006

Title
Windows and doors – Resistance to wind load – Classification
Windows and doors – Resistance to repeated opening and closing – Test method
Windows and pedestrian doors – Mechanical durability – Requirements and classification
Shutters, external blinds, internal blinds – Terminology, glossary and definitions
Shutters and blinds – Additional thermal resistance – Allocation of a class of air permeability to a product
External blinds – Performance requirements including safety
Shutters – Performance requirements including safety
Shutters – Acoustic insulation relative to airborne sound – Expression of performance
Blinds and shutters – Thermal and visual comfort – Performance characteristics and classification
Thermal performance of buildings – Calculation of energy use for heating – Residential buildings
Thermal performance of buildings – Calculation of energy use for heating – Residential buildings
Thermal performance of buildings – Transmission and ventilation heat transfer coefficients – Calculation method (ISO 13789:2007)
Thermal performance of buildings – Heat transfer via the ground – Calculation methods (ISO 13370:2007)
Energy performance of buildings – Calculation of energy use for space heating and cooling (ISO 13790:2008)
Thermal insulation products for building equipment and industrial installations – Determination of declared thermal conductivity (ISO 13787:2003)
Thermal insulation – Determination of steady-state thermal transmission properties of thermal insulation for circular pipes (ISO 8497:1994)
Thermal insulation for building equipment and industrial Installations – Calculation rules (ISO 12241:2008)
Hygrothermal performance of building equipment and industrial installations – Calculation of water vapour diffusion – Cold pipe insulation systems
Building materials and products – Hygrothermal properties – Tabulated design values
Hygrothermal performance of buildings – Calculation and presentation of climatic data – Part 1: Monthly means of single meteorological elements (ISO 15927-1:2003)
Hygrothermal performance of buildings – Calculation and presentation of climatic data – Part 4: Hourly data for assessing the annual energy use for heating and cooling (ISO 15927-4:2005)
Hygrothermal performance of buildings – Calculation and presentation of climatic data – Part 5: Data for design heat load for space heating (ISO 15927-5:2004)
Ventilation for buildings – Design criteria for the indoor environment
Ventilation for buildings – Tests procedures and measuring methods for handing over installed ventilation and air conditioning systems
Ventilation for buildings – Tests procedures and measuring methods for handing over installed ventilation and air conditioning systems
Ventilation for buildings – Symbols, terminology and graphical symbols
Ventilation for buildings – Calculation methods for the determination of air flow rates in dwellings
Ventilation for buildings – Performance testing and installation checks of residential ventilation systems
Ventilation for buildings – Design and dimensioning of residential ventilation systems

SIA no.	Prefix	EN no.	WI no.	Year
382.211	EN ISO	13791	00089062	2004
382.212	EN ISO	13792	00089044	2005
382.251	EN	13142	00156031	2004
382.701	EN	13779	00156057	2007
384.101	EN	12828	00228002	2003
384.105	EN	14337	00228004	2005
384.201	EN	12831	00228012	2003
384.301	prEN	14335	00228013	2005

Title
Thermal performance of buildings – Calculation of internal temperatures of a room in summer without mechanical cooling – General criteria and validation procedures (ISO 13791:2004)
Thermal performance of buildings – Calculation of internal temperatures of a room in summer without mechanical cooling – Simplified methods (ISO 13792:2005)
Ventilation for buildings – Components/products for residential ventilation – Required and optional performance characteristics
Ventilation for non-residential buildings – Performance requirements for ventilation and room-conditioning systems
Heating systems in buildings – Design for water-based heating systems
Heating systems in buildings – Design and installation of direct electrical room heating systems
Heating systems in buildings – Method for calculation of the design heat load
Heating systems in buildings – Design and installation of direct electrical room heating systems

BUILDING CATEGORIES AND STANDARD USES
SIA 380/1, annex A, table 24

Building category		Uses (examples)
I	Apartments Multi-family housing	Multi-family housing, retirement homes, hotels, hostels, childrens' and youth centres, homes for disabled people, drug rehabilitation centres, barracks, prison
II	Apartments Single-family housing	Detached and semi-detached houses, holiday bungalows, terraced houses
III	Administration	Private and public office buildings, ticket halls, doctors' surgeries, libraries, workshops, exhibition halls, cultural centres, datacentres, TV stations, film studios
IV	Schools	School buildings of all levels, kindergartens and day care centres, training rooms and centres, conference buildings, laboratories, research institutes, leisure facilities
V	Shops	Sales rooms of all kinds, including shopping malls, exhibition centres
VI	Restaurants	Restaurants (including kitchens), cafeterias, canteens, dance halls, discotheques
VII	Halls	Theatres, concert halls, cinemas, churches, funeral halls, auditoriums, assembly halls, sports halls, large sports arenas
VIII	Hospitals	Hospitals, psychiatric clinics, nursing homes, rehabilitation centres, surgeries
IX	Industry	Production halls, commercial buildings, assembling halls, service stations, railway stations, fire stations
X	Storage	Warehouses, distribution centres
XI	Sports buildings	Gymnasiums, indoor tennis centres, fitness centres, dressing rooms
XII	Indoor swimming pools	Indoor swimming pools, saunas, health spas

GENERAL CHART FOR VALUES OF STANDARD USES
SIA 380/1, annex A, table 25

Number	Building category		I Apartments, multi-family housing	II Single-family housing	III Administration	IV Schools	V Shops	VI Restaurants	VII Halls	VIII Hospitals	IX Industry	X Storage	XI Sports buildings	XII Indoor swimming pools
3.4.1.1	Interior temperature	θ_i [°C]	20	20	20	20	20	20	20	22	18	18	18	28
3.4.1.2	Area per person	A_P [m²/P]	40	60	20	10	10	5	5	30	20	100	20	20
3.4.1.3	Heat release per person	Q_P [W/P]	70	70	80	70	90	100	80	80	100	100	100	60
3.4.1.4	Time of presence per day	t_P [h]	12	12	6	4	4	3	3	16	6	6	6	4
3.4.1.5	Consumption of electricity per year	Q_E [MJ/m²]	100	80	80	40	120	120	60	100	60	20	20	200
3.4.1.6	Reduction factor for consumption of electricity	f_E [–]	0.7	0.7	0.9	0.9	0.8	0.7	0.8	0.7	0.9	0.9	0.9	0.7
3.4.1.7	Specific external air flow rate	V/A_E [m³/h·m²]	0.7	0.7	0.7	0.7	0.7	1.2	1.0	1.0	0.7	0.3	0.7	0.7
4.3	Heat demand for hot water per year and per TEFA, (thermally enclosed floor area)	Q_{hw} [MJ/m²]	75	50	25	25	25	200	50	100	25	5	300	300

SUBJECT INDEX

APPENDIX

SOURCE OF FIGURES

SIA standards
180 33, 78, 80
180; SN EN ISO 7730 11, 12
180, 1.3.5 69
180, 3.1.3.5 79
180, 3.1.3.3 81
180, 3.1.3.4 81
180, 3.1.4.6 84
180, 4.1.2.2 115
180, A.2, table 13 112, 113
180, A.2, Figure 6 111
180; SN EN ISO 13788 121–127
180/4, Energy need E 102
181 154
181, 2.3 155
181, 2.4 157, 160
181, 3.1.1.2 156
181, 3.2.1.2 155
181, 3.2.1.4, A.2.2.2 156
181, 3.2.2.2 159
181, E.2.1.2, Figure 10 157
181, E.3.1.2, Figure 12 160
181, E.3.2.5, Figure 13 161
SN EN 12207:1999D 82
380/1 78, 84
380/1, 3.4.1.6 84
380/1, annex A, table 24 256
380/1, annex A, table 25 257
381/3 238–241
SN EN 12524; SIA 381.101; 2000 222–231
SN EN 12831: 2003, 82, 83
Documentation D010 19
Documentation D012 17
Documentation D064 242–244
Euronorm; prEN; CEN 14, 15

Federal Department of Home Affairs (FDHA)
Federal Office of Meteorology and Clima-
tology weather data
figs 21, 22, 26, 27

Fasold, Sonntag, Winkler
Bauphysikalische Entwurfslehre, 1987
Verlag für Bauwesen GmbH, Berlin
figs 137, 144–147, 148–151, 152, 167, 173, 177, 179

Noise Abatement Ordinance (NAO)
fig. 138

Handbuch für Beleuchtung
Schweiz. Lichttechnische Gesellschaft
4th edition 1975, Verlag W. Giradet, Essen
figs 189, 202, 203, 206, 207, 209

We would like to thank the SIA (Swiss Association of Engineers and Architects), Huss-Medien GmbH and the publishing group Hüthig Jehle Rehm GmbH, department ecomed security, who have supported and made this publication possible by making pictorial material available free of charge.

APPENDIX

AUTHORS

Bruno Keller

      1972 PhD in physics, ETH Zurich (Swiss Federal Institute of Technology)
1972–1979 High-school physics teacher
1980–1985 Research and development in the construction industry
1985–1990 Management, building up a new business unit for low-energy buildings
1991–2007 Full Professor of Building Physics, Department of Architecture, ETH Zurich
           Academician of the Swiss Academy of Engineering Sciences (SATW)
           Visiting Professor, Southeast University of Nanjing, P.R. China
since 2001 Chairman and co-owner of Keller Technologies AG, with offices in Zurich and Beijing
           Planning and realizing high-comfort low-energy buildings in China.

Stephan Rutz

1982–1988 Studied architecture, ETH Zurich
      1987 Grant to study at Nanjing Institute of Technology, P.R. China
      1988 Diploma (MArch) in architecture, ETH Zurich
1988–1999 Architect in Switzerland and Hong Kong
1996–1998 Design assistant at ETH Zurich
      1999 Joined Chair of Building Physics, Department of Architecture, ETH Zurich
      2000 Founded Rutz Architects, Zurich
2003–2007 Senior assistant in the Chair of Building Physics
      2003 Guest lecturer at F+F School for Art and Media Design, Zurich
2005–2006 Guest lecturer at Southeast University of Nanjing, P.R. China

Pinpoint
Key facts + figures for sustainable buildings
Prof. Dr. Bruno Keller, SIA SPG ASHRAE
Stephan Rutz, dipl. Arch. ETH SIA
Formerly Chair of Building Physics
Faculty of Architecture, ETH Zurich

Contributions:
Iván Antón, dipl. Arch. ETH
Renato Bernasconi, dipl. Arch. ETH SIA
Hannes Gebhard, dipl. Arch. ETH
Florian Guha, dipl. Arch. ETH SIA
Philipp Günther, dipl. Arch. ETH
Dr. rer. nat. habil. Eugen Magyari

Cooperation:
Markus Ettlin, dipl. Arch. ETH SIA
Mirjam Noureldin, dipl. Arch. ETH SIA
Andreas Rubin, dipl. Arch. ETH

Translation:
Prof. Dr. Bruno Keller, SIA SPG ASHRAE
Stephan Rutz, dipl. Arch. ETH SIA

Professional consultant:
Prof. Peter Tagiuri, Rhode Island School of Design

Copy-editing and proofreading:
Monica Buckland, Dresden

Awards:
→ One of the most beautiful German books 2007 –
Category science books.
Buchkunst Foundation, Frankfurt am Main/Leipzig,
Germany, www.stiftung-buchkunst.de
→ Gold Medal – Category edition design.
Joseph Binder Award 2008, designaustria, Vienna,
Austria, www.designaustria.at

Library of Congress Control Number: 2009939318

Bibliographic information published by the German
National Library. The German National Library lists this
publication in the Deutsche Nationalbibliografie;
detailed bibliographic data are available on the Internet
at http://dnb.d-nb.de.

© 2010 Birkhäuser GmbH, Basel
P.O. Box 133, CH-4010 Basel, Switzerland

Original German edition: © 2007: "PINPOINT –
Fakten der Bauphysik zu nachhaltigem Bauen"
by vdf Hochschulverlag AG an der ETH Zürich
English Edition: ISBN 978-3-7281-3313-7

Design and layout concept: Franka Grosse, Zurich
Layout: Anja Denz and Franka Grosse, Zurich
Cover design: Stephan Rutz, Zurich
Info charts: Anja Denz, Esther Hostettler, Zurich
Final drawing: Stephan Rutz, Esther Hostettler, Zurich

Printed on acid-free paper produced from
chlorine-free pulp. TCF ∞

Printed in Germany

ISBN: 978-3-0346-0120-7
9 8 7 6 5 4 3 2 1

www.birkhauser.ch